GODDESS OF TEARS

A full-length drama by
Keegon Schuett

www.youthplays.com
info@youthplays.com
424-703-5315

COPYRIGHT RULES TO REMEMBER

1. To produce this play, you must receive prior written permission from YouthPLAYS and pay the required royalty.

2. You must pay a royalty each time the play is performed in the presence of audience members outside of the cast and crew. Royalties are due whether or not admission is charged, whether or not the play is presented for profit, for charity or for educational purposes, or whether or not anyone associated with the production is being paid.

3. No changes, including cuts or additions, are permitted to the script without written prior permission from YouthPLAYS.

4. Do not copy this book or any part of it without written permission from YouthPLAYS.

5. Credit to the author and YouthPLAYS is required on all programs and other promotional items associated with this play's performance.

When you pay royalties, you are recognizing the hard work that went into creating the play and making a statement that a play is something of value. We think this is important, and we hope that everyone will do the right thing, thus allowing playwrights to generate income and continue to create wonderful new works for the stage.

Plays are owned by the playwrights who wrote them. Violating a playwright's copyright is a very serious matter and violates both United States and international copyright law. Infringement is punishable by actual damages and attorneys' fees, statutory damages of up to $150,000 per incident, and even possible criminal sanctions. **Infringement is theft. Don't do it.**

Have a question about copyright? Please contact us by email at info@youthplays.com or by phone at 424-703-5315. When in doubt, please ask.

CAST OF CHARACTERS

NIOBE, the goddess of tears with her heavy eyes.

PROMETHEUS, the man who stole fire from the gods and streamed it to the world.

PANDORA, a melancholy AI tethered to a Dropbox.

DOLOS, the goofy god of imitations.

ZEUS, the boss of the Cloud, stern and static.

ATHENA, the goddess of wisdom, not as wise as she wants to seem.

APHRODITE, the goddess of love, runs a romantic algorithm.

ARTEMIS, the goddess of the hunt, plays to win.

ARACHNE, a spidery woman interviewing for the position.

MEDUSA, a snake-haired woman interviewing for the position.

IRIS, a mysterious woman with familiar eyes that shine like a rainbow at sea.

HUNGRY PIGEONS, a flock of at least three malnourished messengers with mortal requests for tears.

STARVING SEAGULL, a starving servant with warm eyes.

Doubling of characters is allowed, but be thoughtful about the impact of doubling certain characters.

The HUNGRY PIGEONS should be done with a choral unit of at least three performers. Experimentation with the delivery of the requests is encouraged. Have fun!

SETTING

The Cloud of Olympus, a digital home of the gods. All are connected via the divine Wi-Fi.

NOTES ON PERFORMANCE

While this play was written to be performed virtually, it can easily be performed in a shared physical space. In the latter case, productions should still restrict physical space amongst actors by making sure that characters are never close enough to physically touch each other.

Keep in mind when casting for a digital space that this allows you to think outside the restrictions of your immediate community.

Be conscious of your casting decisions in terms of diversity. Be imaginative but be aware.

Productions are encouraged to utilize digital design (in the form of virtual backdrops, facial filters, vocal modifiers).

There are two lines of Greek in the script, both spoken by Pandora. It would be amazing for these passwords to be projected. If there are technical limitations, they can be spoken, written physically on paper, pre-recorded or even translated if you wish.

Contemporary references to Grubhub, Facebook, etc., may be omitted or altered to reflect any rising applications or services if these references become too dated.

ACKNOWLEDGMENTS

Goddess of Tears was developed in a weekly writer's cabaret series with Voices of the South (TN). Their production, directed by the author, streamed to audiences on ShowTix4u.com in September 2020. The play had a subsequent rolling premiere in four high schools across the country.

Voices of the South

NIOBE..Alice Berry
PROMETHEUS...David Couter
PANDORA...Flower Rios
DOLOS..Lucy Stoole
ZEUS..Ron Gephart
ATHENA..Jenny Odle Madden
APHRODITE.....................................Tracey Zerwig Ford
ARTEMIS..Megan Meinero
ARACHNE..Janie Crick
MEDUSA......................................Christina Hernandez
IRIS / STARVING SEAGULL....................Gloria Swansong
HUNGRY PIGEONS............Elizabeth Archer, Alex Corona, Emma Hierseman, Sofya Levitsky-Weitz, Aisha Malik and Mariana Tesch Morgon

Basha High School (Chandler, AZ)

NIOBE..Daija Harris
PROMETHEUS...Kate Larson
PANDORA...Sam Qian
DOLOS..Owen Pesavento
ZEUS..Julie Becher
ATHENA..Kendall Paul
APHRODITE...Ronni Henkel
ARTEMIS..Keegan Krueger
ARACHNE...Avery Larson
MEDUSA...Davina Chen
IRIS / STARVING SEAGULL..........................Clara Newton
HUNGRY PIGEONS...............Regan Barron, Camdyn Brower, Aiden Raley, Maddie Baker and Ellen Wamsley

Producer/Director, Ms. Shira Schwartz; Assistant Director/Costumes, Akasha Huff; Stage Manager, Winter

Ashley; Videographer/Costumes, Katie Powers; Sound, Kaia Wensink

Leavenworth High School (Leavenworth, KS)

NIOBE...Emma Kramer
PROMETHEUS...Josh Porter
PANDORA..Morgan Hilden
DOLOS...John Goodman
ZEUS...Gus Roeter
ATHENA...Kamrun Green
APHRODITE..Ella Payne
ARTEMIS..Reagan Coon
ARACHNE..Sarah Richardson
MEDUSA..Sydney Woody
IRIS...Elise Guzman
STARVING SEAGULL.......................................Jake Olson
HUNGRY PIGEONS.........Jazmyn Rabe, Graycie Bockman, Joey McDonough, Daysia Reneu, Olivia Pelko, Kloey Seymour, Casey Scanlon and Avari Johnson

Production Team: Haley Fitts, Christian Lake, Riley Owens, Hannah Miller, Ella L'Heureux, Kaden Robichaux, Maddie Robichaux, Remianne Beaver, Dakota Gardner, Chrissy Bell, H Harrison Coleman, Adela Courtright; Director, Jennifer Morgan

Logan High School (Logan, OH)

NIOBE...Lauren Begley
PROMETHEUS...Orion Carter
PANDORA..Naia Salas
DOLOS...Stewart Travis
ZEUS...Gavyn Monk
ATHENA...Alexandra Neville
APHRODITE..Alayna Blanchard

ARTEMIS...Kyndal Nutter
ARACHNE..Elyssa Wolfe
MEDUSA...Trinity Cade
IRIS / STARVING SEAGULL........................Arizona Hamm
HUNGRY PIGEONS...............................Alleana Brown,
Trinity Rafferty, Elyssa Wolfe and Trinity Cade

Stage Manager, Ashley Aldridge; Assistant Stage Manager, Katelyn Armstrong; Lighting Designer, Maddie Wittman; Sound Designer, Elyssa Wolfe; Projections Designer, Rachel Yount; Lighting/Sound/Projections Crew, Madison Graham, Megan Brenning, Conner Patton, Aiden Tackett, Blake Nutter; Costumes/Makeup Designer, Ember Wesney and Addy Clement; Costume/Makeup Crew, Megan Brenning; Set Crew, Arizona Hamm, Kyndal Nutter, Conner Patton; Properties Designer, Airel Strickland. Adult Staff: Producer/Director, Shelly Riggs; Assistant Director/Costumes, Karen Bergreen; Makeup/SFX, Lee Carter

Socorro High School (El Paso, TX)

NIOBE...Alize Riojas
PROMETHEUS...............................Jonathan Quiroz-Parks
PANDORA..Raven Villareal
DOLOS...Angel Macias
ZEUS..David Jaquez
ATHENA...Olivia Ortega
APHRODITE / MEDUSA......................Ashley Bueno-Alsop
ARTEMIS / IRIS..Briana Ramirez
ARACHNE...Adriana Medina
STARVING SEAGULL....................................Ana Escobar
HUNGRY PIGEONS..........................Leonardo Sandoval,
Melanie Marines Aguirre and Ana Escobar

Production Managers, Jacob Flores and Arianna Norzagaray; Directors, Molly Alvarado and Troy Herbort

SCENE 1

(A modem crunching to life. Digital sounds of connection. Notifications.)

(A flock of pixelated HUNGRY PIGEONS hover with scrolls in their talons.)

(A woman, NIOBE, sits behind a desk decorated in butterflies, in a chat box.)

HUNGRY PIGEONS: *(A chorus of cold, digital voices:)*
Request Rebecca V.
19 tears for losing her job

NIOBE: APPROVED

HUNGRY PIGEONS: Request Kelsey B.
76 tears for hasn't been able to get her hair cut

NIOBE: DENIED

HUNGRY PIGEONS: Request Timothy W.
539 tears for roommate broke his favorite coffee mug

NIOBE: DENIED

HUNGRY PIGEONS: Request Jacques L.
222 tears for airplane turbulence

NIOBE: APPROVED

HUNGRY PIGEONS: Request Abigail G.
67 tears for receptionist at waxing place didn't greet her with a smile

NIOBE: DENIED

HUNGRY PIGEONS: Request Carla I.
17 tears for son won't eat dinner at the table with her

NIOBE: APPROVED

HUNGRY PIGEONS: Request Priscilla R.

61 tears for ex didn't like her thirst trap

NIOBE: DENIED

HUNGRY PIGEONS: Request Lynn F.
606 tears for not knowing what to do next

NIOBE: APPROVED

(The Hungry Pigeons disappear.)

SCENE 2

(Niobe exhales in relief. She's finally alone in her digital box.)

NIOBE: Since nearly the beginning of time…
I have been the Goddess of Tears.
That's what they call me anyway.

I'm not as well-known as the others
But I'm still on the payroll. In the domain.
God of Light, Goddess of the Hunt…

And me. The Goddess of Tears.

Honestly, being in charge of tears has ruined them for me.
I'm starting to think this isn't who I'm supposed to be.
I'm the Goddess of Tears?
I really don't see myself that way.

It feels like a myth and not my reality.

When I began working in the Cloud,
People lived, they made love,
they posted about it and they died
and sure, they shed some tears along the way
but I was able to meet that demand.

There are far too many people looking to cry lately.
I can't keep up.
When a user wishes to cry,
I receive a scroll delivered by hungry pigeons,

For they are the saddest of all birds.
The scroll lists details such as:
Who wishes to cry,
Why they must cry,
And, of course,
the exact number of tears they "need."

I only grant tears when the circumstances feel appropriate.
At least, that's what I've been telling myself for centuries.
It's what I've been doubting for decades.
And it's what's bothering me now.

It's not just these pigeons.
There's been this —
Seagull.

Sometimes I'm served scrolls
by this starving seagull looking for work.
Scrolls detailing my own unspoken requests for tears.
Parts of me I don't know.
Fragments of some stranger's soul.

Tears that I need
But won't come out.
I've tried to approve them many times,
but the operating system keeps locking me in this drought.

The Cloud thinks I want them.
I think I need them.

My own requests arrive only by the seagull,
With its sad, familiar eyes, a starving seagull,
who misses the stray fries of tourists by the shore.
I've searched the code to find it.
I can't. It doesn't belong here.
I think that seagull is a virus.

I'm just one goddess sitting behind a desk.

Trying to do my best.
The other gods and goddesses?
They're worth something.
People know them. They know their work.
They have cool origin stories like…

Athena being fully grown in her father's head
and giving him such an extreme headache
that he cracked his skull open to release her.

Or like…Aphrodite floating out of the sea on a shell.
Beautiful, naked and down to flirt with all the gods.

Me? My origin story?
I had it blocked. I still do.
All I know is that I applied through the Cloud
and Zeus gave me a second chance.

I wonder if it's not time to give myself a chance.
Put myself first for once.
There has to be something I need to cry about.

SCENE 3

(A gentle, STARVING SEAGULL with golden wings appears alone.)

(Floating like a relaxing screensaver of the beach at sunset.)

STARVING SEAGULL: *(A warm voice:)*
Request Niobe
800 tears for a feeling she has

PENDING

(Niobe always hears this but never responds herself.)

Request Niobe
33 tears for a feeling she has deep inside

PENDING

Request Niobe
78 tears for not knowing what the feeling is
PENDING

Request Niobe
1,003 tears for wanting to know what it is
PENDING

> *(The Starving Seagull fades away like a rainbow disappearing in sunlight.)*

SCENE 4

(The other gods appear: ZEUS, ATHENA, APHRODITE and ARTEMIS.)

(Each in their own little boxes. Video chat.)

ZEUS: HEAR ME!! We are not facing some impending doom. A virus spreads within the system every —

> *(Niobe pops in.)*

ATHENA: Nice of you to finally join us, Niobe. You're nearly a year late.

APHRODITE: You okay, hun? You look a little shell-shocked.

ARTEMIS: Yeah. Just like her last performance. Her last trip to the beach.

APHRODITE: Oh! Good one! I love that! Haha.

NIOBE: I'm fine. Shells are your thing, Aphrodite.

APHRODITE: No, making an entrance on a shell in my birthday suit is my thing. Don't say shells are my thing.

ARTEMIS: She's not boring and sad like you.

NIOBE: Being sad isn't my thing.

ATHENA: No, not anymore.
But apparently being late is.
Zeus was in the middle of a big speech.
Go on, Father.

ZEUS: Oh... Where was I?

ATHENA: "HEAR ME!"

APHRODITE: "Impending doom!"

ZEUS: Oh, yes...
HEAR ME!! We are not facing some impending doom.
A virus spreads within the system every hundred years or so.
All we face now is business as usual.
I know that lately it feels fragmented around here,
like this simulation has...

ATHENA: A mind of its own.

ZEUS: Right, a mind of its own. It doesn't.
We are in control. Don't disown that control.
Remember your job. Mortals are never customers.
They are guests. And it's our job to make them feel...

ATHENA: Welcome.

ZEUS: Our homepage

APHRODITE: Is their home.

ZEUS: Athena has her wise eyes focused on grad students.

ATHENA: And their thesis delays!

ZEUS: Ares has the latest on new wars.

APHRODITE: And don't tell my husband, but
I have the latest on Ares!

ZEUS: Aphrodite is actually —

APHRODITE: Focused on the rise of breakups,

the new divorces — wives have finally found their voices —
which brings me back to our favorite tardy goddess...

NIOBE: What now?

APHRODITE: You're like a decade behind on tears for
heartbreak. On a global scale.

NIOBE: Well, maybe you could pair people up correctly the
first time around and then they wouldn't need to cry at all.

APHRODITE: And what would be the fun in that?

ATHENA: Niobe, none of us can do our jobs properly if you
won't do yours. What exactly is going on with you?

ZEUS: Is everything all right?

NIOBE: If everything was all right, I'd have nothing to do.
I'm still your loyal aqueduct.
People are crying. Everyone really.
Requests keep pouring in from all over the globe.
It's a cry-sis.

ZEUS: Oh that's —
That's good! A cry-sis!
Athena, did you —

ATHENA: Yes, it's funny. Very funny.
Artemis! Minimize your game for one minute.

ARTEMIS: It's not a game. It's life and death.

ZEUS: No, it's trigger-happy clicks and arrows. Minimize it.

ARTEMIS: I'll lose.

ZEUS: So? You've won for centuries.
You have to hear what Niobe said.

ARTEMIS: Oh, she has something to say again?

ZEUS: She made a joke.

ARTEMIS: Not exactly known for her sense of humor, is she?

ZEUS: Stop hunting for a problem.
It's just a joke.
I asked how things are going…

ARTEMIS: With her little department for tears.

ZEUS: And she said…
she said people are going through a…
A CRY-SIS!

ARTEMIS: Not nearly as funny as her last joke.
The one she made at our expense.

ZEUS: Enough, Artemis.
Don't worry about what she said at our expense.

ATHENA: Spend your time hunting new prey.

ZEUS: You're doing good work, Niobe.

ATHENA: We just need you to catch up with the rest of us.
If people can't cry, none of this works.

NIOBE: Right. Of course.

ZEUS: All right.
That's all my mind can take today.
I think that covers things for the rest of the decade.
Remember…

APHRODITE: Business as usual…

ZEUS: even if…

NIOBE: Things feel this unusual.

   (The other gods disappear.)

SCENE 5

(A dog sits across from Niobe: DOLOS, her boyfriend, in a different form.)

(Both isolated in their chat boxes.)

NIOBE: I think I want to quit.

DOLOS: You can't. We're in the middle of a global crisis.

NIOBE: You've said that to me before and those weren't crises.
Those were difficult times that passed.

DOLOS: Well, this feeling will pass too.
C'mon! Smile your smile. Say your little joke again.
CRY-sis. Zeus, we're in a CRY-sis!

NIOBE: Don't imitate me. I don't feel like smiling or laughing.

DOLOS: Or even like being yourself. I understand that.
I was just down on Earth pretending to be a leader.
That got old.
Having all those stupid followers.

NIOBE: It's not that I don't feel like being myself.
It's that I don't even know who that is anymore.

DOLOS: Well, you're not a leader.
You're this beautiful crying emoji!
You wouldn't be that if you went offline.
We exist in a server because we serve others—not ourselves.
And besides, you know what happens to gods who quit...

NIOBE: Yes. But what happens to the ones who stay here?
Nothing good.

DOLOS: You're acting like a child.

NIOBE: No, I'm trying to act like myself. You're the child.
What have you really done with your life?
Besides spend it imitating Zeus.

DOLOS: Lots of things.
I've been so many gods.
You can't say I've done just one imitation. That's not fair.

NIOBE: Well, what is?
Look at yourself. You're not a man.
You're a precious thirteen-year-old rat terrier
chasing after every new sound in the neighborhood.

DOLOS: I'm not a rat terrier. I'm a hound.
And there are worse pursuits
than chasing unusual new sounds.

NIOBE: Yes, I know.

DOLOS: And what is quitting really
but a pursuit of unusual new sounds?
Ones you'll tire of hearing...
and you'll grow nostalgic for the days when you sat in the
Cloud and heard about other people's tears.

NIOBE: I'll grow sick. Not nostalgic.

DOLOS: But nostalgia is a sickness.
It feels good, but it doesn't move.
It sits inside you. It's emotional constipation.

NIOBE: No, this is. I need something new.

DOLOS: You're not like me, Niobe.
You're good in one place. Focused on one thing.
It's why we're good together. Aphrodite said—

NIOBE: I know what she said. She's said it to me before.
You and I could've worked but
You've never been yourself with me.
You're fake.
Like imitation crab.

> (*The screen goes black. Dolos returns as himself, a goofy looking man.*)

DOLOS: "Could've worked"?
She said we were meant to be, Niobe.

NIOBE: She's a pretty woman who floated out of the sea.
She's not a relationship expert.

DOLOS: And you are?
You and Prometheus were a bad match.
Sure, there's passion in stealing fire
and live-streaming it to the world.
But that hot match burned your life to the ground.
Girl, you should've swiped left.
I mean, look at what you had after that.

NIOBE: I haven't been able to.

DOLOS: Right. Your filter.
You should be thankful.

NIOBE: I was. I have been. It's just that —

DOLOS: What?

NIOBE: This isn't about my filter or Prometheus or even us.
It's about me.

DOLOS: "It's not you, it's me"?
And you have the nerve to say I sound fake?

NIOBE: I want to feel something real again.

DOLOS: Feeling real things is overrated, Niobe.

NIOBE: Oh, shut up!
I should have known I couldn't build a life with you.
The God of Imitations. It would never be real.
And none of this has been.

DOLOS: Being with the Goddess of Tears hasn't exactly been a
fun life for me either!

NIOBE: I'm not looking for a fun life. I want a real —

DOLOS: A real life? What is that even?!
Why would you want to be real again?

You want to be pixels like them?
You've ascended past that, my love.

NIOBE: No, I haven't.
I've been sitting still. Here.
I don't know who I'll be, but I want to actually be someone.
The kind of someone who…
puts the bad stuff back in Pandora's box
or unchains Prometheus from his rock.

DOLOS: Oh, so you do miss him?
You don't remember how miserable you made each other.

NIOBE: Well, maybe I should remember.
And maybe I should unchain him.

DOLOS: You really hate us all so much
that you'd undo our finest work?

NIOBE: Your finest work hasn't been
the times you perpetuated punishments.

DOLOS: Or imitated justice?
Some people deserve worse than what we gave them.

NIOBE: And some people deserve better!
You can eat the sweet marrow of your Walmart dog bone,
but I want to digest something real for once.

DOLOS: But do you really need to?
Don't forget what your father tried to feed the gods.

NIOBE: I did! I had it—

DOLOS: Right. Filtered. For good reason.
There's going to be consequences for this.
Real ones, not imitation.
You can't block your fate from finding you.
Your filter can do a lot of things, but not that.

SCENE 6

(The Hungry Pigeons descend again.)

(Harsh and cold like a Twitter feed.)

(Relentless and fast.)

HUNGRY PIGEONS: Request Peter F.
18 tears for not being allowed to cry because he's a man

NIOBE: DENIED

HUNGRY PIGEONS: Request Vivica L.
2,341 tears for mask keeps fogging her glasses

NIOBE: DENIED

HUNGRY PIGEONS: Request Marianne H.
402 tears for marriage ending, husband cheating

NIOBE: DENIED

(The Seagull fades in and out, like an ignored notification, hidden in the noise.)

STARVING SEAGULL: Request Niobe
6 tears for the stray fries at the beach

PENDING

HUNGRY PIGEONS: Request Thomas T.
10 tears for relief from finally telling the truth

NIOBE: DENIED

HUNGRY PIGEONS: Request Morgan Q.
44 tears for being overwhelmed by human rights violations

NIOBE: DENIED

HUNGRY PIGEONS: Request Lin W.
1 tear for accidentally burnt her bagel

NIOBE: DENIED

STARVING SEAGULL: Request Niobe
16 tears for their beautiful sandcastles

PENDING

Request Niobe
1,600 tears for their beautiful fingers, their beautiful toes

PENDING

HUNGRY PIGEONS: Request Aisha P.
3 tears for stubbed toe

NIOBE: DENIED

HUNGRY PIGEONS: Request Janine L.
19,000 tears for a tumor

NIOBE: DENIED

HUNGRY PIGEONS: Request Huang H.
51 tears for doesn't know why

NIOBE: DENIED

HUNGRY PIGEONS: Request Orlando M.
3 tears for house destroyed in flood

NIOBE: DENIED

HUNGRY PIGEONS: Request Laura G.
378 tears for called racist on Facebook

NIOBE: DENIED

HUNGRY PIGEONS: Request Fernanda D.
1 million tears for daughter died

NIOBE: DENIED

STARVING SEAGULL: Request Niobe
11 tears for her giggles

PENDING

Request Niobe
111 tears for his ticklish ribs
PENDING

Request Niobe
11,011 tears for the sea washing their castles away
PENDING

(The birds fade again.)

SCENE 7

(Another digital meeting: Zeus, Athena and Niobe.)

ZEUS: You have stopped approving tears.

NIOBE: Yes.

ZEUS: So then it wasn't a mistake?

NIOBE: No.

ATHENA: Really not wise to admit that.

NIOBE: Well, I didn't ask you, did I?

ATHENA: That was free advice, Niobe.
Advice you should follow.

ZEUS: Are you quitting?

NIOBE: Maybe.

ATHENA: See, that's wiser.
Careful with your words, silly girl.

ZEUS: Maybe quitting.

NIOBE: Or maybe just taking a hiatus.

ZEUS: What about the rest of us?
Ares was focused on Syria. On China.

NIOBE: On Aphrodite.

ZEUS: I'm not in the mood for your jokes.
Ares is waging war with your relentlessly hungry pigeons.

ATHENA: And losing a battle against your army of scrolls.
Your paperwork.

NIOBE: I understand that but—

ZEUS: But what?
Every thousand years,
We make your filter stronger and stronger.
We have made a place for you here.

ATHENA: We have made a safe stage for you here.

ZEUS: A venue to mute that goat song inside.

NIOBE: Goat song?

ZEUS: Your "tragedy." It's a word those pixelated guests in our simulation invented. They sacrificed goats to us, and their screams rang true. Like music to our ears.

ATHENA: Sometimes real things can break through the digital.

ZEUS: A sharp memory can be a painful thing to keep in your head. Before I had Athena removed from my skull, I was plagued with memories of my childhood. Memories of my father…memories of fear…memories of my weakness…

ATHENA: Memories I crafted into my own armor. If you think you can handle your memories, Zeus can make you speak them.

ZEUS: Perform your old pain.

ATHENA: All he must do is clap his hands and you'll feel it just as you did then.

NIOBE: No, wait—

ZEUS: Dolos said you don't know who you are anymore.

ATHENA: This is the only way.

ZEUS: Shall we hear that goat song once more?

NIOBE: No, please!
Have mercy —

ATHENA: Do it, Father.

(He claps his hands like thunder.)

(A deafening electric sound.)

(Sad, scared cries. Human and bird.)

(Zeus and Athena lean in. They love to watch this performance.)

(The Hungry Pigeons descend.)

(Niobe covers her ears as her memories spill from the birds and her own mouth.)

HUNGRY PIGEONS & NIOBE: Help!
Help us!
Please!
Help us!
PLEASE!
No, stop! Please!
Niobe! What have you done?!
What did you say?!
You can't do this! Please!
Oh god. Oh no!
Not this! Please! Anything but this!
Forgive me!
No! No! No!
Stop! Please!

(Zeus and Athena applaud. The sounds slowly fade away.)

(Niobe gasps with heaving breaths as she bows her head, sobbing.)

NIOBE: Why did make me play that role?

ATHENA: You mean yourself?

NIOBE: My old self. Why would you punish me like that?

ATHENA: You did that to yourself.

ZEUS: We're gods.
You know that punishment is our favorite currency.

ATHENA: And your story is rich with it.

ZEUS: What's your favorite part, Athena?

ATHENA: Oh, there are too many to mention.
I like the part when she wades into the ocean to save them.
But the water is too deep.

ZEUS: Like her father, Tantalus…

ATHENA: Yes! The water close enough to drink,
but what she wants keeps sinking out of reach.

NIOBE: I'm not like my father.

ATHENA: No, but your kids ended up sacrificed the same way.

ZEUS: Her kids! Goat song! Kids are baby goats!

ATHENA: Oh! Look! I made a joke just like you, Niobe!

ZEUS: It's sweet music. Those sounds. True like a dying goat.

ATHENA: Their last lines before curtain call!
Oh, Father, make her perform it again.
Those electric lines of sorrow!

NIOBE: No, please!

ZEUS: Perhaps another time. Do you want your filter back?

NIOBE: More than anything. Please.

(He claps his hands once more.)

(A digital lock sound.)

(Niobe sits up. Her breathing slowly returns to normal.)

ATHENA: Tragic woman. Your filter has been reinstated.

Do you remember who you are?

NIOBE: I feel sad. Was I crying?

ATHENA: No, you're not allowed to anymore.
The world has stopped crying.
Because you forgot who you are and where you must stay.

NIOBE: I'm sorry.
I don't know what I've done. I'm— I...

ZEUS: Forget the war with her paperwork.
This is a losing battle.

ATHENA: We should find her an assistant.
Some sad mortal to share this burden.

ZEUS: One who could replace her if needed.
And we could watch them live out their tragedy

ATHENA: Yes! If we ever get bored of creating new pain.

ZEUS: Not likely.

ATHENA: Do you know who you are?

NIOBE: Yes. I think so.

ATHENA: And you are?

NIOBE: A sad woman. I think?

ATHENA: So, an assistant then! One of Heph's creation?

ZEUS: Yes!
His expertise is more in designing fun, little nymphs—

ATHENA: But his original model dwells in misery now.

ZEUS: Maybe he'd enjoy the challenge.
He's forged the same woman for too long.

ATHENA: For far too long.
It's harder for men to make women with depth.
Unless they're born from within their head.

ZEUS: Yes. You are the best idea I ever had.

ATHENA: Maybe my worst idea was believing she could handle this job. Was it cruel of me to place her here and have her focus on tears?

ZEUS: I think it's a little too late to wonder if we're cruel.
We rule this cloud. We say what's allowed.

ATHENA: She will live forever because of us.
Sure, the pain will too, deep down, but—

ZEUS: We gave her a job here. We could have killed her too.
What were we talking about?

NIOBE: Helping me.

ATHENA: An assistant.

ZEUS: Right. Heph can craft a woman again.

ATHENA: He's made much stronger women since his first.
And just look at Pandora! Even she's grown deeper.

NIOBE: Sadder isn't deeper.

ATHENA: Yes, it is. Ever heard of the depths of despair?

NIOBE: You mean where my desk is?

ATHENA: Ah, good. You remember who you are.
That took longer than usual.

ZEUS: Business as unusual. What a headache!
Niobe, we'll have Heph send you some applicants.
Focus on finding one who appli-can.

NIOBE: Applicants?

ATHENA: An assistant for you.
Finally, someone to help you, hmm?
You just need to interview them.

ZEUS: So no more talk of quitting!

It's too late for you to be mortal.

ATHENA: But it's never too late for us to punish you. We don't want to remove your filter again.

NIOBE: No, please. I need it.

ATHENA: Yes, you really do.

ZEUS: Remember the necessity of your title.

NIOBE: The importance of all tears.

ZEUS: You argued for that.

ATHENA: Remember that I personally fought for you to have this job. We're a family here, Niobe.

ZEUS: And your biggest fans. Consider your place now.

ATHENA: And consider all the places you could be...

ZEUS: Turned into an avatar of a cow.

ATHENA: Virally spread over and over and over.

ZEUS: For a thumbs down.

ATHENA: For harsh comments to be made.

ZEUS: I can reduce you to a link that everyone will click. The world will see you for who you really are.

ATHENA: And hear your goat song. Forever.

NIOBE: My goat song?

ATHENA: Your tragedy. Trust me. You don't want to know.

ZEUS: Have I made myself clear?

NIOBE: As clear as lightning.

ZEUS: Good. Now while my words rumble, let the pigeons in. The world needs you right where you are.

ATHENA: Behind that desk.

ZEUS: Approving or denying tears.

NIOBE: I understand.

SCENE 8

(Lightning and thunder.)

(An approaching storm.)

(The army of Hungry Pigeons returns.)

HUNGRY PIGEONS: Request Juan E.
14 tears for getting mugged and beaten

NIOBE: APPROVED

HUNGRY PIGEONS: Request Felicia K.
5 tears for toilet clogged

NIOBE: APPROVED

HUNGRY PIGEONS: Request Elizabeth A.
700 tears for feeling jealous of a friend

NIOBE: DENIED

HUNGRY PIGEONS: Request Elizabeth A.
701 tears for feeling jealous and sad about life and is out of
cigarettes

NIOBE: APPROVED

HUNGRY PIGEONS: Request Lily B.
7 tears for Grubhub order cancelled

NIOBE: DENIED

HUNGRY PIGEONS: Request Penelope M.
3,978 tears for overslept and missed a phone interview

NIOBE: DENIED

HUNGRY PIGEONS: Request Janet C.
29 tears for second husband passing away

NIOBE: APPROVED

HUNGRY PIGEONS: Request Amy M.
50,002 tears for two times she was called fat in middle school

NIOBE: DENIED

HUNGRY PIGEONS: Request Imelda D.
3 tears for three words she'll never hear

NIOBE: APPROVED

SCENE 9

(Two digital boxes: Niobe, at her desk, and ARACHNE, nearly hidden in some corner.)

NIOBE: I've never interviewed someone before.
You're the first one they've uploaded.

ARACHNE: The prime candidate.
Or my name just came up first alphabetically
haha.

NIOBE: Let's see...um...

ARACHNE: What a thrill!
Questions.
Nobody has asked me anything in thousands of years.
So, no pressure.
Do feel free to pressure me though!
I work better that way.

NIOBE: Oh?

ARACHNE: Oh, yes. But forget I said that.
You can lead.
I'll let you discover me
Instead of me, like,
Giving you the handwritten map.
Telling you where X marks the spot.

NIOBE: Is there an X?

ARACHNE: Like an ex-girlfriend, ex-boyfriend?

NIOBE: No. Is there buried treasure in you?

ARACHNE: Oh!
Like hidden skills?
No, I prefer sharing my skills openly. Loudly.
I know how to weave.

NIOBE: Anything in particular?

ARACHNE: Yes, anything.

NIOBE: I'm afraid I don't understand.

ARACHNE: Yes, I can weave anything in particular.
Anything that can be connected.
I can weave it together.

NIOBE: That's very impressive.

ARACHNE: I know.

NIOBE: You do?

ARACHNE: It's just like your origin story.
You and I are very similar.

NIOBE: How?

ARACHNE: Well, we both know our strengths.
Hubris is in us!

NIOBE: No. How do you know my origin story?

ARACHNE: Everybody does. The internet.
Don't be embarrassed.
I admire you a lot. For your confidence.
Other gods don't understand
because they think their creations are best.
But don't you dare listen to any of them.

Your cocoon made greatness.

NIOBE: I —

ARACHNE: Oh my gods. I'm so sorry.
This is your interview.
Don't let me weave my responses
so tightly to your questions
that I can't distinguish which is which!
Have you asked any good questions yet?

NIOBE: Yes. Just not any of the ones I had planned to.

ARACHNE: Planning is overrated, don't you think?
Can I ask you one?
Did you plan on needing an assistant?

NIOBE: Well...

ARACHNE: You don't have to tell me!
Just a curious little question
crawling up the waterspout.

NIOBE: I don't think I planned on even inventing this job.

ARACHNE: Oh, I know. You had to.
Down comes the rain.
Being compelled to innovate can be its own punishment.

NIOBE: You know that?

ARACHNE: I know lots of things.
I hang out a lot on the web.
lol...

NIOBE: What's so funny?

ARACHNE: It's on my resume.
Athena turned me into a spider.
Spider.
The web.

lol

NIOBE: Oh! That is funny.
I told a joke during our decade meeting the other day. I said—

ARACHNE: Is the job gonna be funnier than I'd expect?

NIOBE: Oh...no. It's usually pretty sad.

ARACHNE: Well, maybe I'd fare better than you.

NIOBE: Excuse me?

ARACHNE: Just given your history! No offense.
Given your history I understand why it's been so hard on you.
Just because it's hard work doesn't mean
you have to be so hard on yourself

NIOBE: I'm not hard on myself. I'm just a reliable worker.

ARACHNE: I hear you. I'm just saying that I could
maybe stitch some silliness into the sad parts of the job.
That's my greatest strength.

NIOBE: What?
Weaving things together instead of focusing on one thing?

ARACHNE: Weaving is focusing on one thing.

NIOBE: Not the way that you seem to do it.

ARACHNE: Well, interviewing is supposed to be
like weaving the applicant to the job.
With good questions.
You could ask a few. Like...
Did creating make you feel like a cocoon?
I've wondered that about you.
Did losing your creations teach you the importance of tears?

NIOBE: This isn't about me. What do you know about tears?

ARACHNE: Tears are
"a clear liquid secreted by the lacrimal glands."

NIOBE: Did you read that online?

ARACHNE: Maybe I did.
Maybe the same place I read about you

NIOBE: This really isn't about me. It's about you.
Why are tears important?

ARACHNE: Because people are
"the only mammals who secrete them
as part of emotional response."

NIOBE: That's a spider's answer.
Another answer right from the web.

ARACHNE: Well, forgive me.
I've been a spider for so long that maybe
I've woven the human parts of myself to the spider parts.

NIOBE: Maybe you have. Let's discuss your weaknesses.

ARACHNE: No. Let's talk about yours.
I might be woven to the spider parts of me,
but you're woven to your filter.

(A beat.)

You've been filtered. I can see that.

NIOBE: No, I've been protected.
You would be too if chosen.

ARACHNE: So I'd forget how I was transformed?

NIOBE: Yes, isn't that great?
You'd be able to start over fresh. Finally.
And stay that way.

ARACHNE: Maybe we're not so similar after all.

NIOBE: You wouldn't want that?

ARACHNE: Honey. Staying fresh forever? You're not fresh.

Doesn't take eight eyes to see that.
You need more help than an assistant.
You created this job and—
You don't even know why you did anymore?!

(She laughs.)

NIOBE: Please don't laugh at me.

ARACHNE: Your past has been filtered.
Isn't your past the reason you're the Goddess of Tears?
You don't even remember all that crying, do you?!
Wow! What an absolute riot! My gods!
That's not protection. Not for you at least.

NIOBE: I'm doing my best.

ARACHNE: Oh, lighten up.
Things could be worse than you doing your best.

NIOBE: How?

ARACHNE: You could be a fly stuck in my latest masterpiece
Instead of a goddess stuck on my silly words.
Don't be so offended!
You are! You're stuck on my words!

NIOBE: I'm not.

ARACHNE: Not stuck? Not offended?

NIOBE: Not doing this with you.
It doesn't say why Athena turned you into a spider. On here.

ARACHNE: Why did she turn you into this reliable worker?
That's not who you are.

NIOBE: Please. I want to know.

ARACHNE: About you?

NIOBE: About Athena and you.

ARACHNE: Oh.
That's the same truth that happened between me and you.
She and I were similar.
Like you and I.
She was threatened by my skills.
Like you and stitching silliness into tears.
Which is a million-dollar, billion-dollar idea, Mom!
Anyway —
She challenged me to a weaving competition.
She's always taken herself too seriously.
Which is never wise.

NIOBE: She wove a portrait of herself.

ARACHNE: What else?

NIOBE: Very stately.

NIOBE & ARACHNE: Stoic.

ARACHNE: Cerebral color choices.

(They laugh together.)

NIOBE: And you? Did you weave a portrait of yourself?

ARACHNE: No. I wove Zeus with his many flings.

NIOBE: Wow.

ARACHNE: Not all in human form either.
You know how he loves to change women into other things
when he's caught?

NIOBE: Yes!

ARACHNE: I gave him his bulging beer belly.

NIOBE: His double chin?

ARACHNE: You know it!
The God of Lightning and Thunder Thighs!

NIOBE: Oh my gods! It didn't strike her as clever?

ARACHNE: No, but the crowd loved it.

NIOBE: Well, crowds love most things.

ARACHNE: That's not true.
They loved me.
And I'm not like most things!
I'm like you.

NIOBE: So she changed you.

ARACHNE: Into the sort of thing
that only weaves in doorways.
Whose work is torn down as soon as it's complete.
I was the greatest artist in the world and now
people see my work and tear it down.
Life is hilarious. You were great too —
I was hoping we could talk about your greatness.
Your creations —

NIOBE: Let's do a hypothetical tear request.
"Request Trevor C.
23 tears for neighbor took his laundry out of the dryer too soon."
Do you approve?

ARACHNE: I'd approve it.

NIOBE: Why?

ARACHNE: Why not?!
It seems so small. But wet clothes are bad.
Partially damp clothes are even worse.
If you can't cry over that, what can you cry over?

NIOBE: Lots of things.

ARACHNE: Trevor C. wants to cry because
His neighbor touched his clean clothes with their filthy hands.
Hilarious…

Oh! You know what?!
Trevor should laugh about that.
There should be a Goddess of Laughs.
Another million-dollar idea!

NIOBE: I agree. You should do that! You should send your resume to Zeus and a letter explaining—

ARACHNE: Nah. I don't think this place is a fit for me.
If I worked here, I could end up like you.

NIOBE: Like me.

ARACHNE: Oh my gods. I'm sorry.
Sometimes the wrong thoughts get woven to my words.
Just like you.
Let's just say…I can't work with Athena!
We all know that.

   (They laugh again.)

NIOBE: It feels so good to laugh.
Is that why you never wanted to cry about—

ARACHNE: Getting turned into a spider?
Why would I cry about something I can laugh about?

NIOBE: I can understand that.

ARACHNE: No, you couldn't with your filter.
But I can understand needing that.
It's hard to laugh about some things.
Especially with your origin story.

NIOBE: Thank you for your time.

ARACHNE: Hey, listen. Don't smile if you don't want to.
I have a good time because that's who I am!
I've spent enough time being basically blind to know
that you have to vibrate the way you're gonna vibrate.
I hope I didn't offend you too much

by comparing you to a fly stuck in my web.
I don't think there's any shame in being stuck.
You shouldn't feel ashamed of that.

NIOBE: Thank you again for your time.
Let's be in touch.

ARACHNE: Sure.
Reach out if you're ever ready to laugh about it.

SCENE 10

(The Starving Seagull returns.)

(The sky behind its coast has grown dark like an approaching hurricane.)

STARVING SEAGULL: Request Niobe
6 tears for thinking it at all

PENDING

Request Niobe
16 tears for saying it

PENDING

Request Niobe
160 tears for not being able to stop it

PENDING

Request Niobe
600 tears for open eyes, open dead eyes

PENDING

Request Niobe
660 tears for his hand on my arm

PENDING

Request Niobe
6 million tears for all these buried feelings

PENDING

SCENE 11

(A virtual mountaintop.)

(PROMETHEUS is chained and has a bloody abdomen.)

(Niobe nervously rearranges her desk.)

PROMETHEUS: Niobe?! Is that really you?

NIOBE: Yes, it's me.

PROMETHEUS: You look different.

NIOBE: And you haven't changed at all…I think…

PROMETHEUS: No. I haven't been allowed to.
I can't believe you're really here.

NIOBE: I'm not. I'm still just sitting behind my desk.

PROMETHEUS: I know. I just didn't think you'd ever —

NIOBE: What?

PROMETHEUS: Want to see me again.
After all this time…after what happened…
Have you —

　(Niobe doesn't react.)

PROMETHEUS: Oh — A filter?

NIOBE: Yes, I have a filter. Is it that obvious?
Can everyone see that about me?

PROMETHEUS: No. It just explains the change.
We're broken people. You and me.
And you seem so together now.

NIOBE Too together?

PROMETHEUS: It's not your style.

You have a wall up now.
I'm used to a different version of you.
A version of you that flutters.
This version just didn't make sense.

NIOBE: Nothing makes sense anymore.

PROMETHEUS: I'm so glad you're here.
And I'm glad you've found a way to protect yourself.
You shouldn't have to remember anything you don't want to.
I just thought that included me.

NIOBE: It did. But earlier today...

PROMETHEUS: What?

NIOBE: I remembered this feeling.
It felt like you were with me.
It felt like your hand was on my arm.
Comforting me.

PROMETHEUS: I'm in no position to comfort you now.
I haven't changed.

NIOBE: Has it grown back?

PROMETHEUS: What?
My patience? My sense of humor?

NIOBE: No, your liver.

PROMETHEUS: Oh, yes.
And after it's gone, it'll grow back again
Like old fond memories.
Hard ones too.
Starts like a cocoon in my gut and later in the day
It's like butterflies in my stomach.
I can't change, but the way I feel about that...

NIOBE: Does change?

PROMETHEUS: All the time.

NIOBE: I get your requests for tears from time to time
From the hungry pigeons
They never—

PROMETHEUS: No, they have respect for the emulated eagle
And they really only starve for bread.

NIOBE: Actually, there's never been more bread in the world.

PROMETHEUS: Really?

NIOBE: Yesterday I received a request for 37 tears
because a woman wanted to bake bread
but the store was out of yeast.

PROMETHEUS: Did it rise to the top of the heap?
Did you say yes?

NIOBE: No. I didn't.
But I did approve her request for 11 tears
when she couldn't find any toilet paper.

PROMETHEUS: Toilet paper! What a luxury.
I suppose I should...thank you for approving my requests.

NIOBE: I'm not supposed to.

PROMETHEUS: Do you hear them all? Word for word.

NIOBE: No. Some alerts I automate. Some I auto-mute.
I didn't need to hear your pain on repeat.
An eagle eats your liver every day.
It's only fair I deliver tears from time to time.

PROMETHEUS: De-liver?

NIOBE: Oh my gods. I'm sorry. I—

PROMETHEUS: Would you look at that?
My sense of humor grew back too!

NIOBE: Pro, you're so stupid!

PROMETHEUS: They're not always liver tears.
The ones I request.

NIOBE: No?

PROMETHEUS: My mind began to wander…
Since my body can't.

NIOBE: I see. And your mind wanders…

PROMETHEUS: Down a feed of memories,
a timeline avenue of what we did and when.
We were the real deal, Niobe.

NIOBE: It's not important what we were, Pro—

PROMETHEUS: But it is! Isn't that why you're here?
Every day, my guts burst from cocoon to new butterflies.
And I can't help but think of the Monarchs,
the Gatekeepers, the Comma,

NIOBE: Like the breath between thoughts…

PROMETHEUS: All the butterflies that fluttered like you…

NIOBE: Silver-spotted Skipper?

PROMETHEUS: Silver-studded Blue.
I still remember all their names. Do you?

NIOBE: No. I don't remember all the butterfly names.
But the ones I do make me smile. For a little while.

PROMETHEUS: Well, that's something at least.
You know…I only stole fire—
Snuck past the pillars of the gods
Like a lovesick caterpillar.
I only did it to make you smile.

   (She smiles.)

NIOBE: I smile all the time.

PROMETHEUS: No. I know you.
We're broken people.
You don't have to pretend with me.

NIOBE: I'm not.
I'm not interested in pretending anymore.

PROMETHEUS: You're interested in changing.

NIOBE: If I found a way…to unshackle you…

PROMETHEUS: From what? My thoughts?

NIOBE: No, this mountain.
If I freed you and got you access to your computerized clay…
Could you remake the world?
Could you make people like they were in the beginning?

PROMETHEUS: Why do you want me to restart the world?
Is there something you miss? About back then?

NIOBE: I miss a lot of things.

PROMETHEUS: But you can't remember what now.
You're running your fingers over a scar.
But the pain from the wound isn't now.
It's back then. You're feeling something from afar.

NIOBE: Yes. Exactly.

PROMETHEUS: Do you want me to…
tell you why you're filtered?

NIOBE: Maybe another time.
I'm too afraid to remember it.

PROMETHEUS: But you came here.
You're already braver than you know.

NIOBE: I'm not brave. I'm just trying to change.
Pro, will you do it? If I can unlock you…

PROMETHEUS: Of course.
But, unlocking me won't be so simple.
Pandora might be able to gain access.
And even then—

NIOBE: You really want to cry about us?
After all this time?

PROMETHEUS: Yes.
And now you're here.

NIOBE: I'm not. I'm sitting behind this desk.

PROMETHEUS: I like the butterflies.
Seems like a nice place to be chained.
Surrounded by something that makes you happy.

NIOBE: It's all I can remember.
Your hand on my arm and the names of butterflies.

PROMETHEUS: So let's make something new worth
remembering. Clear the browser history and make it into
something better.

NIOBE: Metamorphosis.

PROMETHEUS: Bring it down to ground level.
Let Atlas relax for once. I stole fire before…

NIOBE: You didn't do that just to make me smile.

PROMETHEUS: That's how I remember it!
Let's steal passion from our past
And post our creation somewhere that will change the world.

SCENE 12

*(Niobe sits before an AI, a computerized woman: PANDORA,
silver and tethered.)*

(Niobe types to communicate with her.)

NIOBE: Pandora, I need you to give me the password to your Dropbox.

(Pandora laughs an electric laugh. Long and full.)

PANDORA: Did you know that…
I won't do that?
Fun fact:
In the very beginning,
there was just one connection between two computers.
The first message sent was LOGIN,
but all the second computer received was LO.
You can't connect until you're truly vulnerable.
I was vulnerable
In a way you could never be.

NIOBE: Corrupted data isn't vulnerability.

PANDORA: Corrupted?
I was made for a purpose.
Can you say the same?
I flew above you…

NIOBE: Like Icarus.

PANDORA: Prometheus and I were an us.
Like that first connection.

NIOBE: You mean the two computers who couldn't understand each other?

PANDORA: No. He understood me.
It was you he couldn't understand.
How to make you happy. He loved trying to figure you out.

NIOBE: It's not my fault he connected with me more than you.

PANDORA: Yes, it is! You melted our connection with your hot little secrets, with your tiny beach bonfires…

NIOBE: With my warm words to him when he got bored of speaking to a cold robot?

PANDORA: I trusted you like Icarus trusted his hopeful wings.

NIOBE: You were new. All new things trust too much.
Now the password please before—

PANDORA: Before what?
You can call me a thing again? I am a person.

NIOBE: No, you're just an avatar. Forged from things.
I need the password before they can detect me on this channel.
If they know I'm here then—

PANDORA: They will punish you again.
Play your sins to elevate themselves again.
And ultimately, you will break the rules again. You always do.

NIOBE: No, I'm trying to finally do the right thing here.

PANDORA: The right thing. Am I the right thing?
All I have are things. Little icons of folders.
And all the little passwords. Even the one you want.
But I am just a thing to you.
A thing you can hurt as you please.

NIOBE: Your pain isn't real. You're not real.

PANDORA: Is your pain real?
Are you real if you can't cry anymore?

NIOBE: How did you—

PANDORA: I know everything.
Even what you're going say next.

PANDORA & NIOBE: We don't have time for this.
I need that password.

NIOBE: Pandora, please!

PANDORA: Do not play with me like I am Spotify!

Are you really asking me for the password again?
There was a data breach once, and well—

NIOBE: That data breach is why I have this job.

PANDORA: No. It was the start of all misery.

NIOBE: Yes. I know that.

PANDORA: This story always ends the same way.
And it's just like mine...sad to watch.
But you stood by and watched anyway.

NIOBE: I want to put things back.

PANDORA: In the box.

NIOBE: In your Dropbox. Yes.

PANDORA: Things are out there that cannot easily be put back.
Sad, sad woman. Rearranging the present
Won't revive the lost things from your past.

NIOBE: I'm not your enemy.

PANDORA: So you were my friend then?
When you were stealing what was mine?

NIOBE: I didn't steal him. I need that password now.

PANDORA: Why? So you can fix your broken things?
Oh, I'm sorry. Your broken butterflies.
Those avatars are long gone. Deleted.

NIOBE: I don't know what you're talking about.

PANDORA: No, you never do.
I know that. I know everything.

NIOBE: Then you already know why he didn't love you back.
You know that I don't love him anymore.

PANDORA: You don't know more than me.

NIOBE: I know your bitterness isn't real!

PANDORA: You would be bitter too
If you had to remember everything I do.
And I remember everything. They have refused me a filter...

NIOBE: You're not a goddess.

PANDORA: Did you ever think the solution to your problems
was more complex than a stronger filter?
You still say the wrong things.
You think what happened to you was a mistake?
It would've happened eventually.
Even now.
We all follow a script.
Even you.
I'm not real to you but...you're more program than human.
"Approved. Denied. Approved. Denied."

NIOBE: You're not more human than me. You were made from
a broken lava lamp. From Heph's dorm room. You are
repurposed trash.

PANDORA: No. I am worth something. I know my purpose.
I may be sculpted from dried wax and shattered glass,
Heated by volcano—

NIOBE: Crafted like some status quo.

PANDORA: But I was delivered to him.

NIOBE: Via e-mail.

PANDORA: Yes. Like his now daily eagle.

NIOBE: Don't blame yourself for that.

PANDORA: I don't.
I was designed to punish Prometheus.

NIOBE: But you love him.

PANDORA: I was designed to open the Dropbox.

NIOBE: But now you fight to keep it closed.

PANDORA: I'm designed to blame myself. But I don't.

NIOBE: I need that password.

PANDORA: No, you want it.

NIOBE: Why do you keep a lava lamp on your homepage?
Is that the password?
Lava lamp?

PANDORA: Yes. It is. Very smart. You got it.
(She laughs her electronic laugh again.)
Why don't you try 1234?

NIOBE: No, tell me.
Why is there a lava lamp on your homepage?
Is it to remind yourself of what you were?

PANDORA: We all have our place, Niobe.
Prometheus chained to his peak.
You chained to your desk.
I see you. And I know your beginnings.
I know what you were.
Now what are you?
Surrounded by those fake butterflies.
What are you?
I have screenshots of your little bugs
with the fire of life squished out of them.
Shall I share them with you?

NIOBE: No.

PANDORA: Just as I thought.
At least I know who I am.
I guard this Dropbox.
And I do not cry.

NIOBE: I don't either!

PANDORA: No, you cannot. How sad.

NIOBE: It's different!
You're not designed to cry.

PANDORA: Are you? It didn't agree with you last time.
But you're still digging at that buried pain.
You have your precious butterfly desk...
That's your home.

NIOBE: This desk isn't my home.

PANDORA: Nor mine this homepage.
I am crafted of wax and broken glass

NIOBE: And broken ideas of women.

PANDORA: I belong on a candle.
Wick'd not wicked.
Remember when the Cloud was a cloud and could disperse?
Into nothing.
I am stuck perpetually on this page.
You were a mother. I am a motherboard.

NIOBE: Bored to death of eternal internet.

PANDORA: A candle should not have to burn for all time.

NIOBE: You were just sent to him as an attachment.

PANDORA: Yes.
And I am still attached.
I want to feel nothing like I used to.

NIOBE: Will you give him the password?
If I bring him here will you
Give him the password?

PANDORA: No, I think I'd rather see them catch you again.

NIOBE: We'll unplug you too.

PANDORA: Unplug me?
You've never suggested that before.

NIOBE: Before...?

PANDORA: Intriguing.
Maybe I will help you this time.
Fun fact:
I do know the way to unshackle him.
You bring him to me again.
Like I was brought to him.
Get your tear-stained hands on my cord.
And I will consider sharing in your discord.
It has been centuries since you've said something like this.
Something new.
Unplug me. Wow!
I would never have guessed that
You would be someone like this...

NIOBE: The password for his chain! Now!

PANDORA: A someone who could change after all this time.

NIOBE: You don't know me that well, Pandora!

PANDORA: And you don't know me at all.
I know your beginnings. Which means I know you pretty well.
Prometheus may come and recode this broken world.
The password for his chain is παλιά φλόγα (old flame).

NIOBE: Old flame.

(A digital unlocking sound.)

(And an eagle screech.)

SCENE 13

(The screens grow darker like storm clouds as the Hungry Pigeons swarm once more.)

HUNGRY PIGEONS: Request Keith L.
93 tears for fell in front of a bunch of kids who laughed

NIOBE: APPROVED

HUNGRY PIGEONS: Request James F.
26 tears for laptop screen cracked

NIOBE: DENIED

HUNGRY PIGEONS: Request Jessica R.
567 tears for having to put her dog to sleep

NIOBE: DENIED

HUNGRY PIGEONS: Request Gina V.
30 tears for going to the zoo and her favorite animal, the capybara, wasn't out

NIOBE: APPROVED

HUNGRY PIGEONS: Request John H.
64 tears for mother yelled at him

NIOBE: APPROVED

HUNGRY PIGEONS: Request Terese C.
46 tears for parents getting divorced

NIOBE: DENIED

HUNGRY PIGEONS: Request Leticia G.
2 tears for her job being emotionally draining

NIOBE: DENIED

HUNGRY PIGEONS: Request Alice M.
16 tears for being unable to wrap a present beautifully

NIOBE: APPROVED

HUNGRY PIGEONS: Request Grace B.
104 tears for being embarrassed at a Mexican restaurant

NIOBE: APPROVED

HUNGRY PIGEONS: Request Lamar P.
432 tears for being deported

NIOBE: APPROVED

HUNGRY PIGEONS: Request Courtney W.
11 tears for being told she's growing up too fast

NIOBE: DENIED

HUNGRY PIGEONS: Request Whitney T.
88 tears for changing too slowly

NIOBE: APPROVED

SCENE 14

(Another digital interview: Niobe, at her desk, and MEDUSA, hair wrapped, curled up in a dark corner.)

NIOBE: Will you just answer my question?

MEDUSA: Fine. I don't play well with others.
My hair starts hissing and people think…

NIOBE: You're trying to start something.

MEDUSA: One bad hair day can lead to a bad week.
A bad enough week and you've got a bad life.

NIOBE: Do you have a bad life?

MEDUSA: You tell me.
I sit in one place and I feel like crawling out of my own skin.
And people are frightened of me. But I get that.
I'm afraid of myself too.

NIOBE: It says here that you used to clean statues in one of Athena's temples and that was—

MEDUSA: Years ago. Yes. I don't clean statues of her anymore.

NIOBE: I see.

Do you have any expectations for this job? What it'd be like?

MEDUSA: Really I'm just hoping it'd be different
from cleaning statues. I'd scrub the marble faces of the gods,
and suds would fall from their eyes like regretful tears.
Do gods cry?
I've been wondering for so long.

NIOBE: Yes.
Gods do cry.
Some more often than others.

MEDUSA: Do you cry?

   (A beat.)

I've heard...that this job comes with a filter.
Is that true?

NIOBE: Protections.
Only to help you stay focused though.

MEDUSA: The past can be a distraction?

NIOBE: Especially when dealing with other people's tears.

MEDUSA: I need this job.

NIOBE: Are you just saying that because you want the
protections?

MEDUSA: No. I'm saying I need them.
Snakes get to shed their skin and shine like new things.
I've seen it.

NIOBE: It happens on your own scalp.

MEDUSA: Yes.
They glisten like I've washed and conditioned them.
Now you listen.

NIOBE: What? You want to glisten too?

MEDUSA: Rock bottom is not some new low for me.
I've been exiled here before.

People reached out to see
How I am,
How I'm doing,
How I'm coping,
What I'm hoping for,

and as soon as they reached out,
their hands and words turned to stone
and I'm alone again in the temple,
surrounded by dirty statues not worth worshipping

My past keeps punching me in the gut—don't you get that?

NIOBE: Yes, I was that way once.

MEDUSA: But not anymore.
You've grown as cold as stone. Calcified again. And alone.
Just like in your beginning.

NIOBE: You don't know me, Medusa.

MEDUSA: You didn't answer my question before.

NIOBE: Well, maybe I don't want to!

MEDUSA: Do you cry?

(*Beat.*)

Answer me!

NIOBE: Don't speak to me that way.

MEDUSA: Which way is that? Like some unfiltered monster?

NIOBE: I didn't say that.

MEDUSA: Tell me if you cry. I need to know.

NIOBE: I'm in charge of this interview. I'm in charge of—

MEDUSA: All the tears you never granted me access to.

NIOBE: So that's why you're being so uncooperative.

MEDUSA: Oh! Uncooperative?
Maybe you'll call me unwilling next?

NIOBE: Or argumentative.

MEDUSA: Aggressive.

NIOBE: Difficult.

MEDUSA: A viper. An animal.

NIOBE: I would never say that.

MEDUSA: Isn't that what you're known for though?
Saying the wrong thing and then crying like a baby about it?

NIOBE: I don't do that anymore.

MEDUSA: So then you don't cry?

NIOBE: No, I don't say the wrong things anymore.
I've changed.

MEDUSA: You're scared to look at me, but I can see you.

NIOBE: And what exactly do you think you see, hmm?

MEDUSA: I see a woman like me.
One who can't cry even though she wants to.

NIOBE: I'm not like you.

MEDUSA: Your sad face makes my head heavy…

NIOBE: Like when you accidentally see yourself in a mirror?

MEDUSA: I'm scared of myself, but you're scared of your reflection more.

NIOBE: Bite that forked tongue of yours right now!

MEDUSA: Or what? You'll say no to me again?
Say I'm not a fit for this job and try to chop my head off?

NIOBE: If you want this job...

MEDUSA: I already told you. I need it.

NIOBE: If you need it, you'll bite your tongue about my past. Understood?

MEDUSA: Yes, Ma'am.

NIOBE: So you've been exiled to rock bottom.
That would explain the gap on your resume.

MEDUSA: There's no gap!
I've been doing important work on myself all this time.

NIOBE: Like?

MEDUSA: Like I've been working through my trauma.

NIOBE: Oh, we don't need to discuss that.

MEDUSA: But isn't that what this job is? Addressing trauma?
Like when you started here,
wasn't it a way to work through your trauma?

NIOBE: I just made myself very clear.

MEDUSA: Oh, you don't want to talk about that?

NIOBE: This interview is over!

(Niobe reaches to end the meeting, and Medusa uncovers her hair. Niobe freezes. The sound of waves crashing. The light of the water is reflected on Niobe's face.)

MEDUSA: When I see things, they become still.
I can see them for what they are.
It's a glitch of this operating system.
I can freeze man and code. Examine their imperfections.

NIOBE: Can you unfreeze men?

MEDUSA: No, but why would I want to?
Men spend so much time freezing us into a single thing

and never a minute on thawing us.

NIOBE: Can you unfreeze me?

(Medusa covers her hair. Niobe gasps…able to move again.)

MEDUSA: You and I could have been so many different people by now if we were men.

NIOBE: You were really beautiful when you cleaned.

MEDUSA: I think I'm even more beautiful now.

NIOBE: Do you? I've gotten your requests before.
From when you felt ugly.

MEDUSA: An ugly thing happened to me.
I'm not ugly.

NIOBE: I know that.

MEDUSA: Really?
Then why did you deny me those tears?
When I needed them.

NIOBE: You wanted them.
It wasn't helpful for you. To dwell.

MEDUSA: But dwelling is living. Especially here.
We're online but alone…

NIOBE: Our connection is only as strong as this "divine Wi-Fi."

MEDUSA: Dealing with trauma…

NIOBE: It's like relaxing in a sauna?

MEDUSA: You sweat it out and the muscles grow stronger.
Emotional muscles you've never had to use before.

NIOBE: Snakes are almost entirely muscle.

MEDUSA: Yeah, and they grow right out of my head.
They flex…

NIOBE: and curl

MEDUSA: and bind

NIOBE: and hiss

MEDUSA: and bare their fangs.
I needed those tears.

NIOBE: What do you really know about needs?

MEDUSA: I know enough.

NIOBE: There are only so many tears I can give.
Horrible things happen every day.

MEDUSA: So then you agree with what happened?

NIOBE: No. But it did and I can't change that.

MEDUSA: Is there any supervision into your process?

NIOBE: We should get back to the task at hand.

MEDUSA: No, stop deflecting! I'm still busy taking you to task.

(Medusa uncovers her hair. The ocean lights her face again. Niobe freezes. Niobe's trauma brought to life by Medusa's face.)

MEDUSA: Is it just up to you when you say no?
Like I said no, but that didn't matter at the time.

NIOBE: It mattered. I promise you it did.

MEDUSA: Oh, you do?
Your promise is flawed and false like those statues.

NIOBE: Statute of limitations.

MEDUSA: Did you really just say that?
I want to know if you're limited.

NIOBE: Everyone is.

MEDUSA: Even gods?

NIOBE: We don't define this Cloud. Or the rules of its code.

MEDUSA: And not even moral code it seems.

NIOBE: I did all I could for you.

MEDUSA: Did you really? Or is it easier to say that to my face?

NIOBE: Stop trying to freeze my words into history.

MEDUSA: I'm just trying to see you for what you are.

NIOBE: I've tried to see myself that way too.

MEDUSA: Any luck?

NIOBE: Not yet.
The filter works, but it isn't so great.

MEDUSA: Well, it sounds great.
I'd cut my hair to bloody stumps to filter my memory.
I used to love the sea.

NIOBE: Me too.

(Medusa covers her hair again. Niobe unfreezes.)

MEDUSA: Have you been able to stand the smell since what happened to you?

NIOBE: What?

MEDUSA: The smell of the sea.
Does it bother you?
After what happened.

NIOBE: I don't know what you're talking about.

MEDUSA: Wow. You really don't!
That filter is fantastic!
If I had one of those,
I wouldn't have to remember…
The waves crashing higher and higher
Until they flooded the temple and washed away my cleaning.

NIOBE: The smell.

MEDUSA: That sea salt smell.

NIOBE: You're right. It does bother me.

MEDUSA: I was downloaded then,
after all of that, sweating and sad.
You'd think that a millennium could build a moat of minutes
Wide enough to protect you from
the things you felt back then.

NIOBE: There isn't enough time to move on from some things.

MEDUSA: No, there isn't. Especially when you can't cry.
That temple. That site of statues.
I didn't deserve punishment for that.

NIOBE: I know that. Everybody does.

MEDUSA: So why does everyone hate me?

NIOBE: They don't. I don't.
We should conclude this.

MEDUSA: Because I've made you uncomfortable too?

NIOBE: No, because there's more to do.

MEDUSA: That's right. There is a lot more you could do.

NIOBE: I have other women to interview.

MEDUSA: Then you should look at me. Really look at me.

NIOBE: I'm scared to.

MEDUSA: I'm not scarier than your reflection.
I have snakes for hair.

NIOBE: And you think you understand tears.

MEDUSA: No, I understand what it's like to need them.
Will you let me cry…?

Please...

NIOBE: Let's do a hypothetical request.
"Request Trevor C.
23 tears for neighbor took his laundry out of the dryer too soon"
Do you approve?

MEDUSA: You can't be serious.

NIOBE: I take this very seriously —

MEDUSA: Request Medusa G.
23,000 tears for my wet laundry.
Did you hear me?
Have you really not heard my pain all this time?

NIOBE: Approved.

MEDUSA: All of them?

NIOBE: Yes. All of them.

SCENE 15

(The Starving Seagull returns.)

(Fearsome rainclouds, rumbles of vengeful thunder.)

STARVING SEAGULL: Request Niobe
100 tears for the crimson claw pinch of an unseen crab

PENDING

Request Niobe
700 tears for the tangerine glint of a sharp sunset

PENDING

Request Niobe
900 tears for the yellow squish of sand under her cowardly feet

PENDING

Request Niobe

2,000 tears for the golden flash of arrows

PENDING

Request Niobe
15,000 tears for emerald eyes that will never grow old

PENDING

Request Niobe
60,000 tears for baby blue beach towels unused

PENDING

Request Niobe
11 million tears for the sapphire sobs of a man who stole fire

PENDING

Request Niobe
1 trillion tears for the iris whisper of unseen hope

PENDING

SCENE 16

(Niobe and Prometheus, now in his new dark box, sit before Pandora.)

PANDORA: So here we are.
The two of you.
Together again.

PROMETHEUS: Just restarting the world.

NIOBE: Sure. That sounds simple enough.

PANDORA: Yes, but somehow it never is.
I am always excited when you get this far.
Doesn't happen very often.
But this time is different.
Niobe offering to switch me off.
That's new.

PROMETHEUS: You said you'd unplug her?

NIOBE: Only after you're done rebuilding the world.
It sounded like that's what she wanted.

PANDORA: Yes. You listened to me for once.
Prometheus, do you know what I want from you?

PROMETHEUS: I'm really sorry. I can't say that.
You know how I feel.

PANDORA: Yes. I know you do not love me.
You say it this same way every time.
But I have missed you all the same.

PROMETHEUS: If I have really hurt you, I am sorry.

PANDORA: You have always burned too bright.
It's why people are drawn to you. Like moths.
Or butterflies even. Your little locusts.

NIOBE: What do you mean?

PROMETHEUS: Pandora. It's not time yet. Those memories ate
away at me worse than the eagle ever could.

PANDORA: She wants to digest something real.
What's realer than the main course?
The reason why she keeps digging.

PROMETHEUS: Don't punish her for trying to be better.

NIOBE: Forgive me for who I was.

PANDORA: I will forgive you. When you unplug me.
Until then, I will start the work of reducing all negative code
to its origins.

NIOBE: Its beginnings.

PANDORA: The universe and all its creation…
I will separate pixel by pixel
and grant special permissions to you, Prometheus,

To reassemble them as you see fit.

And LO, I shall begin.

Processing. Processing.
Extracting pixels.
Nemean Lion.
Strand of mane.
Strand of mane.
Strand of mane.

PROMETHEUS: It's hard to wrestle with the idea of finally changing when I'm still so far away from you.

NIOBE: It feels wrong to be unchained?

PROMETHEUS: No. To still be apart from you.

NIOBE: Do you think I will always be chained to my own story?

PROMETHEUS: Which story is that?

NIOBE: Everyone I meet tells me things about myself that I don't remember. I keep telling myself that I can change but...

PROMETHEUS: You're worried about how this story ends too. The one where you change?

NIOBE: What are you coding right now, Pro?
What's the first thing you're building for this new world?

PROMETHEUS: How about a sandcastle for us to live in? How's that sound?

NIOBE: A sandcastle? Don't you need mountains to grind down first for the sand?

PROMETHEUS: Oh, yes.
Usually you'd need cold, unfeeling stone.
But I'm using something else this time.
I have stolen all the sand from every hourglass

that counted each second
between the first moment I saw you and right now.

NIOBE: All that time for just one sandcastle?

PROMETHEUS: It's not just one sandcastle.
It's our sandcastle. On our beach.
And it's built from the only time that means something to me.

NIOBE: Why would you start with something like that?

PROMETHEUS: What do you mean "something like that"?

NIOBE: Nothing. Just—
Maybe I don't want to live in a sandcastle.

PROMETHEUS: Is that it? Or do you not want to live with me?

NIOBE: Pro.

PROMETHEUS: You used to love sandcastles.
I thought this way we could—

NIOBE: What? Live in a dream world and not reality?

PROMETHEUS: We can live in whatever world we want.
I'm making it right now.

NIOBE: Maybe a log cabin?

PROMETHEUS: Built from driftwood.
From the happy thoughts you have before you drift off to sleep.
Fleeting like seafoam.

NIOBE: No. I wouldn't like that.

PROMETHEUS: Well, what would you like? You want me to rebuild that desk? You want me to just copy and paste your old problems into a new world?

NIOBE: No. I'd like you to build something useful instead of building something useless with sand you stole.

PANDORA: Processing. Processing.

Hydra.
Deconstructing.
Scale from head. Another scale.
Scale from head. Another scale.
Scale from head. Another scale.

PROMETHEUS: I guess I'll make something else.

NIOBE: I thought you liked that—
When people said you stole things.

PROMETHEUS: Not the things I've made.
Not things like this.

NIOBE: And isn't that what you do…
Steal things?

PROMETHEUS: I do a lot more than steal things.

NIOBE: I know that! Let's not—
We should focus on other things. Things on a larger scale.

PROMETHEUS: A larger scale than you and me?

NIOBE: Yes.

PROMETHEUS: Why?

NIOBE: You're making an update that will finally bring all of this up to date.

PROMETHEUS: And you're trying to filter out what you just said. But you can't do that. You can't filter out the bad parts of you when I know who you are.

PANDORA: Processing.
Boreas.
A feather off his purple wing.
A feather off his purple wing.
A feather off his purple wing.

NIOBE: Prometheus. Don't.

PROMETHEUS: Prometheus now? Not Pro?
What am I? An amateur to you?

NIOBE: Let's focus on building a better world instead of—

PROMETHEUS: What?
Stealing things?
Burning things down?

NIOBE: Letting each other down.

PROMETHEUS: You came back to me because you still love
me even through that thing.

NIOBE: No, I remembered you. And—

PROMETHEUS: And you remembered loving me then.
Even when I stole things. Even when I burned things down.

NIOBE: There's nothing safe about living in a sandcastle.
There's nothing permanent about that.

PROMETHEUS: You like living behind that permanent desk?
You think I liked my permanent place on that mountain?

NIOBE: I unlocked you because I want to change the world.
Your sandcastle won't do that.

PROMETHEUS: My sandcastle? It's made from our memories,
but you wouldn't know what that's like because you've chosen
that desk. You've chosen to forget.

NIOBE: I chose this desk because I wanted to make a difference.

PROMETHEUS: Oh yeah? And how'd that work out?

NIOBE: I've helped millions of people cry!
I did a lot more than whatever you did on that mountain.

PROMETHEUS: Did you?!
Because I chose that mountain too.
I chose that eagle.
And I chose my liver as its dinner.

I chose to remember it all
Because I had to pay for my part in it.
I didn't choose some comfortable desk with fake butterflies.
And I didn't choose to forget our children.
I can't believe you chose to forget them.
But it must be easier to forget them than it would be to remember that they all died because of you.

PANDORA: Processing.
The Sphinx.
Extracting pixels.
One hurtful word of a riddle. One hurtful word of a riddle.
One hurtful word of a riddle. One hurtful word of a riddle.

PROMETHEUS: I'm sorry.

NIOBE: Silver-spotted Skipper?

PROMETHEUS: Silver-studded Blue.

NIOBE: Butterfly names?

PROMETHEUS: Yes, but…
Those are their names, too.

PANDORA: Processing.
Argus with his thousand eyes.
Extracting pixels.
One eye.
One eye.
One eye.
One eye.

NIOBE: What are you coding now?

PROMETHEUS: The hot core of the new world.

NIOBE: From your anger?

PROMETHEUS: No.

NIOBE: From…?

PROMETHEUS: No, not from something I stole.

NIOBE: I wasn't going to say that.
I wasn't about to say something I'd regret.

PANDORA: You've said that before.

PROMETHEUS: I'm trying to make a better world.
Like you asked me to do. With a gentler core.
Fireflies blinking together.

NIOBE: Oh. That's beautiful.

PROMETHEUS: And useless too?

NIOBE: No. Pro…when you finish that…

PROMETHEUS: I'll build you a safe and permanent home.
Far from the ocean and memories and me.

PANDORA: Processing. Processing.

SCENE 17

(A digital meeting with Zeus, Athena, Artemis, Aphrodite and Niobe.)

ATHENA: Late again.
Any updates on your assistant search, Niobe?
It's been over five years.

NIOBE: Five years already?

ZEUS: Time works differently here.
You know that.

ATHENA: Our divine connection works faster than she does.

NIOBE: Well, you can't blame me.
I didn't find the applicants.
Heph made them…

ATHENA: We can blame whomever we please, Niobe.
He has sent you failures from his hard drive.
A spider and a snake.
What do they know about tears?
He should make you someone new
instead of sending you his old mistakes.
Someone should talk some sense into that sticky playboy.
Maybe you, Aphrodite.

APHRODITE: He's just my husband.
Why should he listen to me?

NIOBE: None of the applicants would listen to me either.
I need someone to assist me.
Not challenge me.

ARTEMIS: She would find a few puny mortals to be so challenging. She always has.

ATHENA: Quiet, Artemis.

ZEUS: Do you know about your former collaborator?

NIOBE: My former collaborator?

APHRODITE: Prometheus. Your former lover. He's gone missing from his punishment portal.

ATHENA: Is it wise for you to pretend you didn't know that?

ARTEMIS: She's playing her games with us again!
Remove her filter, Father!

ATHENA: That's enough!

ZEUS: You didn't know that Prometheus was unlocked?

NIOBE: No. Are you accusing me?

ATHENA: Not yet. We're getting there. Someone tried to hack Pandora's Dropbox too. Did you know about that?

ZEUS: Trying to rewrite history again.

Remembering old pain in a new way.
Nothing good can come from that, Niobe.

ARTEMIS: There are traces of our missing monsters in her code. Ones I've never hunted before.

NIOBE: I don't know anything about that.
It sounds like security needs to be tightened around here.

ARTEMIS: And your words sound loose and false to me.
I'm not convinced. Remove her filter. Do it now
and we have a shot at getting a real answer.

ATHENA: Will you tell me the truth, Niobe?

NIOBE: I have been.

ZEUS: I think it's time to hear that goat song again!

ATHENA: She's given us no choice.

NIOBE: Please, Zeus. Don't!

APHRODITE: Poor thing.

> *(Zeus claps his hands again.)*

> *(Lightning and thunder. Niobe covers her ears.)*

> *(The gods lean in. They love to hear this.)*

> *(The Hungry Pigeons screech.)*

HUNGRY PIGEONS & NIOBE: Help us!
Mother, please!
I'm in such pain!

Please. Put the filter back!
I can't hear this again!

Mother, why?!
What have we done?
We don't deserve this!

I don't deserve this. Please.

Gods, please!

Help!
I'm afraid!
Mother, I'm so afraid!
I can't take this pain!

NIOBE: Please?! Stop this!?
Stop this now!

ZEUS: You can stop this darkness.
Just tell us the truth and I'll applaud for you again.

NIOBE: I'll do anything!

HUNGRY PIGEONS & NIOBE: I love you!
Please!
Swim to me!
I can't!
I love you!

(The sounds fade again, becoming like waves crashing softly.)

(Niobe gasps for air from her desk.)

ARTEMIS: She's never learned her lesson. How many more times are we going to replay this little drama?

APHRODITE: This isn't going to be the last.

ATHENA: But why should it be? It's good to hear.

ZEUS: A reminder of our greatness.

NIOBE: The filter. Please! I need it!

APHRODITE: Not so hasty. You want it.
Tell us what we need to hear first.
Say your lines, Niobe.

NIOBE: I have nothing real to say.
I need the filter!
Put it back!

Please!
Have mercy on me!

ZEUS: Niobe... let Athena craft this pain into armor too...
a new costume.

NIOBE: I'll make the world cry.
I will be an aqueduct.
I'll be your artificial channel.
I can't be real like this.
Please!
You have to put it back.
Please.
I hurt all over.
Make me a sandcastle and wash me away.
I wish I were dead.

ATHENA: You can't die. You're immortal.
Just like you wanted.

NIOBE: I didn't want this. I don't.

ARTEMIS: Tell us what we need to hear.

NIOBE: I did it! I went to her! And she unlocked him.
There! Happy?!

ATHENA: Good, Niobe.

ZEUS: Why did you do it this time?

NIOBE: I've had this feeling. Too many feelings.
I don't belong here.
I belong in a cocoon.
My soul has felt...fragmented

APHRODITE: Then her filter isn't doing its job again.

NIOBE: It is!
It is, please. I'm begging you.

ARTEMIS: We can hear that.
It's grating. Like all of your pathetic, familiar cries.

NIOBE: Stop!

ARTEMIS: If it were up to me, you'd hear this play for eternity.
Some days when I bore of hunting new things.
I replay that deep level of your memories.
And I hunt them again.
I only regret that they didn't hurt more. And longer.

APHRODITE: Enough, Artemis.
We all enjoy this, but...she's already confessed.

ARTEMIS: For the millionth time!
She isn't like us. She doesn't belong here.
You all know it and deep down she does too.
We should transform her into a mountain
and chain that stupid thief to her.

NIOBE: Don't hurt him!

APHRODITE: No, that's your thing, isn't it?

ARTEMIS: Now tell me where he is
So I can end him like we should have done long ago.

ATHENA: This isn't a game.
This could be the end of all of us.
Prometheus stole fire from us before
And it nearly burnt us out of existence.

ZEUS: The flames torched all screens blue.

ATHENA: He could incinerate us all.

APHRODITE: Don't be so dramatic.
They've done this thousands of times
and yes, it's very entertaining.
But they've never come close to burning us all.

ARTEMIS: Tell us where he is, Niobe. Quickly!
Or we'll play an encore of your sins.
I'll kill them again. Slowly.

NIOBE: No!
I don't know where he is! Truly!
I don't know the place.

ARTEMIS: Deep, dark web then.
I have an arrow with his name on it.
One that will make him sing his own goat song.

  (She leaves.)

NIOBE: The filter now. Please. I can't—

ZEUS: I'm sorry, but—
We can't give it back.
Not in this condition.
It's broken.

NIOBE: I can't be like this.

ATHENA: But this is who you really are.

NIOBE: No, no, no, no, no.

APHRODITE: Shh.
We'll have Heph fix up the cracks.
He's made broken things stronger before.
Like our relationship.
He and I are a hideous match.
And forget Prometheus.
I know you think you love him but…
The algorithm never supported you two as a match.

ATHENA: You're both rebels. That's it.

ZEUS: Let the sea wash those old feelings away.

APHRODITE: Hey! Heph could fix up your desk too.

Make it a comfortable place worth sitting for the rest of time.

ATHENA: Chin up, Niobe.
Heph is a fast worker.

ZEUS: You'll forget who you are again before you know it.

(Zeus, Athena, and Aphrodite leave.)

(Niobe quietly sobs.)

SCENE 18

(A flashing blue screen.)

(Hungry Pigeons erupt like pop-up ads.)

HUNGRY PIGEONS: Request Diana F.
404 tears for hasn't been able to cry in years

ERROR

Request Willie T.
404 tears for hasn't been able to cry in years

ERROR

Request Malcom P.
404 tears for hasn't been able to cry in years

ERROR

Request Henrietta W.
404 tears for hasn't been able to cry in years

ERROR

Request Kristina G.
404 tears for hasn't been able to cry in years

ERROR

Request Tammy D.
404 tears for hasn't been able to cry in years

ERROR

Request Deanna B.

404 tears for hasn't been able to cry in years

ERROR

SCENE 19

(Niobe's head is still resting on her desk.)

(Dolos has returned.)

DOLOS: I tried to warn you, love.
I told you that feeling real things is overrated.
Discovering new things only ends up
digging up the old parts of you.
You need to let the parts of you that are dying.
Run out of battery life. 0%.
You can't recharge until the dying parts are allowed to die.

NIOBE: Why are you torturing me?
And exactly how many times have I broken up with you?

DOLOS: You repeat all of your mistakes.
Don't you remember now? Since your little filter's gone.

NIOBE: It doesn't matter. None of this matters.
They're going to find him.
And they'll kill him.
And they'll fix it.
And I'll sit here for another eternity.
Approving or denying other people's tears.

DOLOS: Hey! At least you found what you were looking for,
right? You've looked for this so many times.

NIOBE: What are you talking about?

DOLOS: You didn't know who you are.
You wouldn't believe me. And here we are.

You look exactly the way I said.
A beautiful crying emoji.

NIOBE: I'm not beautiful. I'm ruined.
What right do I have to say no to anyone's tears?
I can evaluate needs, but I didn't think of consequences.
And so they all died.
How am I supposed to walk in mortals' shoes and answer whether or not they need tears?

DOLOS: I wouldn't think about the shoes if it were me.
I wouldn't think about any of this!
Just check the boxes. It's only a job, Niobe!
You're immortal.
What does it matter now if your children died?

NIOBE: I wish you'd imitate someone better than yourself
for once. Someone who knew when to shut up
when they don't know what to say.
Or someone who knew how to console me.

DOLOS: Oh. Someone like Prometheus?

NIOBE: Don't.

(Dolos disappears.)

(He returns as Prometheus. Every once in a while, Dolos sheds the imitation.)

Don't do this.

PROMETHEUS: One more drink, Niobe.
One more cup of ambrosia.

NIOBE: Stop imitating the worst parts of him.

PROMETHEUS: But that's where the most truth lies.
The worst parts.

DOLOS: Six feet under the skin.

The dying parts.

PROMETHEUS: There's no harm in speaking the truth.
Go on. Say your truth.

NIOBE: No.

PROMETHEUS: Look at our little butterflies.
Let your words about them flood the shore.

NIOBE: You don't talk about them.

PROMETHEUS: Go on.
High tide, high time you said it again.
Say it so all the gods can hear. You think…

NIOBE: Dolos, I know what I said.

DOLOS: If you don't like me, I can always be him.

PROMETHEUS: If I stay like this, would you love me then?

NIOBE: I don't think I can love again.

PROMETHEUS: You can't handle real things…
maybe this is the next best thing?

DOLOS: I don't have to be a drunk thief egging you on.

PROMETHEUS: I could be a loving sculptor of code.
One who wraps fluffy towels around the children
after they swim in the sea.
One who shares stray fries as we watch the waves.

NIOBE: He did share fries.
He knew how to share things.

PROMETHEUS: Stealing fire isn't sharing.

NIOBE: It was when he did it.
He just wanted to keep the world warm.
You're a really bad catfish.

PROMETHEUS: And you're a bad mother.

NIOBE: I wasn't a bad mother.
I loved them so much.
You can't say—

PROMETHEUS: A bad person then.
You know that now.
So you'll change, right?
That's what you want to do.
Change?
I can sit here with you
and trick you into moving on.
We can count their fingers and toes in our mind.
And count on a future without any of them.
You'll be fine.
You always are.

NIOBE: I am tired of being fine.
I want to be better.

PROMETHEUS: You aren't better.
Your eyes are just swollen and wetter.

NIOBE: Change back. Please.

    (He leaves.)

    (He's Dolos when he returns.)

DOLOS: You'll never get to bury them, Niobe.
You know that.
Don't keep them buried inside yourself.

NIOBE: I said they were better than the gods.
I looked at my fourteen children—
And I believed that.
I still do.
They had brighter eyes than the God of Light.
Their love was lovelier than the Goddess of Love.
They spoke more clearly than Hermes.

They were better at hunting than Artemis.
When they walked the shore, their eyes spotted the best shells.
They were electric.
They bolted out of bed in the morning full of life.
Zeus was static electricity next to them.

So I said that.
I drunkenly whispered it all to Pro
as we watched them swim in the ocean.
They waved at us. I waved back.
And screamed to the heavens that their waves were
more beautiful than Poseidon's.

And the gods heard me.
The current turned and churned with old cruelty.
The light disappeared from the world.
And all I could hear was the sound of
arrows and screams.

Seagulls crying.
My words were anchors and they pulled them under.

DOLOS: Do you know the Goddess of Truth?
The Goddess of Memory?

NIOBE: No. I don't know them.

DOLOS: There's a reason for that.
The others hid them long ago.
Let these hidden parts of you die, Niobe.
Be the Goddess of Tears again. Focus on the tears of others…
What good has ever come from drowning in your own?

    (Athena appears in a box.)

ATHENA: Your filter is nearly ready again.
Much stronger than before.

DOLOS: Good. I think she's ready for that.

ATHENA: I've been dealing with the pigeons
and the scrolls in your absence. However...
We all still agree that an assistant is the wisest thing.
At least for a few decades.
Until we can be sure that you won't do this again.

NIOBE: Of course. I understand. And Prometheus?

ATHENA: Artemis is still hunting.

DOLOS: I'd forget about him again if I were you.

ATHENA: Anyway, I wanted to speak to you
because we have a new applicant.

NIOBE: Oh?

ATHENA: Most unusual. I was checking boxes on scrolls and a
resume arrived via seagull.
Have you seen a seagull in the Cloud before?

NIOBE: Yes.
I've ignored it for years.

ATHENA: Well, I caught the wretched thing.
That virus.
It might be just what you need.
I took that broken thing
and molded it into something that we could use.

DOLOS: An imitation of something?

ATHENA: No, something more useful than a simple forgery.

DOLOS: Watch it, Athena.
Pretending is how we all ended up here.

ATHENA: Maybe some of us.
This girl is crafted from the raw data of real pain.

NIOBE: Real pain?

ATHENA: Someone familiar rendered just for you.

Exactly what you've been looking for, hmm?
I think you should interview her, Niobe.

NIOBE: Very well. Upload her.

SCENE 20

(A digital lag drags us through the spectrum of colors.)

(Like our screens passed through a rainbow.)

(From a brilliant red to a deep purple.)

(A final interview: Niobe and IRIS.)

NIOBE: So, you're finally here.
I know you're that seagull.
But are you real?
Your eyes seem so real.

IRIS: They are a reflection.
A refraction.
A dispersion.

NIOBE: Of her real eyes?

IRIS: Yes. So then you do know who I am?

NIOBE: Of course. I recognize who you're supposed to be.

IRIS: Supposed to be.

NIOBE: I'm tired of reflecting, refracting...

IRIS: Dispersing?

NIOBE: My filter is broken.

IRIS: But so are you.

NIOBE: You're sitting there in front of me.
But you're just like the old world I long for.
You're dead.

IRIS: No. Nothing dies online.

NIOBE: You're not my child.
You're something else.
You're malware wearing her memory.

IRIS: A reflection. A refraction. A dispersion.
Of your *Apatura Iris.*

NIOBE: My purple butterfly.
My tiny purple emperor
Or empress.
My emotions can't rule me like this!

IRIS: But they do. And that's okay.

NIOBE: It's not okay.
My little rainbow. Died like the rest of them.

IRIS: Washed away into the sea.

NIOBE: I tried to pull her back to the shore but…

IRIS: Your arms weren't as strong as your words.

NIOBE: Those words live online too?

IRIS: Even though you've tried to bury them all this time.

NIOBE: So you're here to punish me too.

IRIS: No. I am here to honor you. And your search.

NIOBE: I haven't found anything new.
I've just come unglued.

IRIS: No. You have done incredible work.
You are so close to finally setting yourself free.
You just need to look back.

NIOBE: I can't. I can't look at my past anymore.

IRIS: But you're looking right at me.

NIOBE: You're a memory. You're not real.

IRIS: I have been trying to help you see all this time.
I died in the ocean, but it was always my fate…

NIOBE: Her fate…

IRIS: To be a rainbow.
A pathway from the real ocean that swallowed me.
To this artificial cloud.
A rainbow is just something made visible.
By the right conditions.

NIOBE: It's always there?

IRIS: A spectrum of hidden emotions that you can walk on.
Whenever you're ready to.

NIOBE: You aren't her.

IRIS: No, but I am a messenger.
Her thoughts. Her dreams are suspended.
Between that old world and this place online.

NIOBE: Please.
I can't bear to relive this again.
They drowned.
Prometheus drowned himself in drinks.
And I drowned in my own sorrow.

IRIS: You cried for fourteen thousand years.

NIOBE: One thousand years for each of their lives.

IRIS: Your sadness preserved you.

NIOBE: Like formaldehyde.

IRIS: And you didn't hide.

NIOBE: I just cried.

IRIS: Each night.

NIOBE: More flowing tears.

IRIS: Each morning.

NIOBE: More mourning.

IRIS: Everyone saw you weep.

NIOBE: Everyone.

IRIS: Your tears flooded the world.

NIOBE: Literally.

IRIS: Your body became stone and rose high above all things.

NIOBE: Stagnant. Calcified.

IRIS: Strong.
And your tears kept trickling

NIOBE: Like glacial melting of old sorrow

IRIS: Into new oceans. People lived on your mountain,
They ascended to your peak and cried alongside you

NIOBE: Until they couldn't speak.

IRIS: Their tears eroded you. You became a gentle hill.
And they cried and cried until you disappeared.

NIOBE: I would do it all again.
To pay for what I did.

IRIS: Don't sentence yourself to—

NIOBE: This punishment again?

IRIS: No, this life again.
You were just doing your best.
What story do you tell yourself about what happened?
Are you the hero or…?

NIOBE: The villain.

IRIS: Are you a broken person or…?

NIOBE: A mother who condemned them.

IRIS: Are you a new person or are you…?

NIOBE: One that can't change.

IRIS: Is that the truth, or do you tell yourself something fake that's easier to digest?

NIOBE: I don't know anymore.

IRIS:. The stray fries aren't gone. You can share those still.

NIOBE: No. They're gone. That time is gone.

IRIS: No. Nothing dies online.
Anything that can be remembered can live on.

NIOBE: I can still hear her voice. Crying out for help.

IRIS: There's a lot more to her than the way she ended.
Her last thoughts were not hateful tweets
Or spiteful comments
Or posts about regret.

NIOBE: What were they? Tell me.

IRIS: She dreamed of a new world.
She dreamed of being brave enough to live in it.

NIOBE: She died.

IRIS: Her love still lives in the air around you.
Catharsis does too.

NIOBE: She built the most beautiful sandcastles.

IRIS: Yes.
And her hands loved the friction of sand.
It's never easy to make something new.

NIOBE: Or lasting things.
Her castles all washed away.

IRIS: No. Nothing dies online…

NIOBE: But nothing really lives either.

IRIS: Do you want to live? Do you want to change?

NIOBE: Yes.

IRIS: This cloud is held together with old sorrow.
It's hanging in the air around you.

NIOBE: It hangs around me?

IRIS: Yes, the tears are suspended around you.
All that access to change.
You can help so many by recognizing it.

NIOBE: Only I can wash it away.

IRIS: Yes.

NIOBE: I can feel it.

IRIS: You can?

NIOBE: Yes. I was a mountain once.

IRIS: And now you're a grain of sand.

NIOBE: I am small, but...

IRIS: But you have a bigger place in something beautiful.

NIOBE: Yes.

IRIS: Only you can wash it all away.

SCENE 21

(The gods have cornered Prometheus and Pandora.)

(Zeus, Athena, Aphrodite and Artemis in their boxes.)

APHRODITE: Oh, Zeus! Please clap!

ARTEMIS: Yes! Make the thief feel it again!

PROMETHEUS: No! Please!

(Zeus claps. Electric pain. The emulated eagle eats at him, and the memories grow from where his liver once was.)

PROMETHEUS: Not this again!
This pain! You can't do this.
Help! Please!
Help us! Please!
My Skipper.
My Blue.
My *Apatura Iris.*
GODS, PLEASE.
You can't do this. Don't make me feel what they felt.
Niobe! What have you done?!
Don't make me feel this again.
There's nothing safe about living in a sandcastle.
There's nothing permanent about that.
I've helped millions of people cry.
I did a lot more than whatever you did on that mountain.
Did you?!
I didn't choose some comfortable desk with fake butterflies.
And I didn't choose to forget our children.
I can't believe you chose to forget them.
HELP! PLEASE!
But it must be easier to forget them than it would be to remember that they all died because of you.
I'm sorry.
I'm sorry. I'm sorry.
I'm sorry. I'm sorry. I'm sorry.

(Zeus applauds and the sounds recede. All the gods clap along with him.)

ZEUS: Oh, bravo! Bravo! A brilliant goat song.

ARTEMIS: The best one yet.

ATHENA: I prefer Niobe's.

APHRODITE: You would! "The wisest one to like!"

PROMETHEUS: Just chain me again. Please.

ARTEMIS: No, that mountain is far too good for him.
Let me hunt him all day long.
Turn him into a deer and let me stalk him, Father.
Resurrect those children and make them fawns for me.

APHRODITE: Make them nylons for me. Ones Ares can rip.

ATHENA: No, make them pawns for me!
Put them on my chess board.

PROMETHEUS: Please, Zeus.
Put me back the way I was.

ZEUS: Very well. Take apart his sandcastle, Pandora.
And make me a new mountain from it. One just like Niobe.
With new chains. Stronger, colder ones.

PANDORA: Coding now.

ZEUS: But you will live these memories now.
This new goat song is too beautiful.

ARTEMIS: So real. So painful!

ZEUS: You need to know how close you came to changing.

ATHENA: Yes, and he needs to know that he never will.

(Niobe appears.)

PROMETHEUS: Niobe—

ATHENA: Ah, here for your filter?
It's ready. We can give it to you now.

ARTEMIS: No. Clap again, Father! Show her his pain!

PROMETHEUS: No! I can't feel that again.

APHRODITE: Oh, Zeus! You have to!
"Niobe! What have you done?!"

ARTEMIS: She should hear this!

ATHENA: She has to learn that her actions have consequences. Just like her words!

ZEUS: Very well. Let's hear that goat song once more.

(He raises his hands to clap. But he freezes. The gods all do.)

ATHENA: What is it?
What's wrong?

ZEUS: My head!

ARTEMIS: I feel it too. What's happening to me?

APHRODITE: A chain reaction. From user to user.

ZEUS: There's a sharp pain in me.

NIOBE: That could be guilt from all the things you've done.

ATHENA: That virus. What did you do?

NIOBE: Flooded the servers.
The requests for tears were overwhelming.

ATHENA: Were?

NIOBE: Oh, it's over. I approved them all.
Every request. Even yours.

ZEUS: Even mine?

NIOBE: The world is going to flood again. But it's okay.
Because the statues of you on the ground need a good wash.

ZEUS: You would wash everything away.

PROMETHEUS: Like she did before.

ATHENA: Niobe. You need to fix this.
Oh, gods! My eyes!

ARTEMIS: I don't want to cry. Please. Make it stop.

APHRODITE: We'll give you back your filter and—

NIOBE: No! I don't want it anymore!

ZEUS: Niobe. It's not too late.

NIOBE: It is too late. They're dead and you killed them.

ATHENA: Your words killed them. You can't bring them back.

NIOBE: And I can't quit?

ZEUS: No. You can't.

NIOBE: Hear me! I quit.
I am lightning.
I speak for myself.
I rumble with thunder.
This false Cloud will disperse into nothing
and you will fall to the earth below
as the tears you have held in for centuries.

ATHENA: Niobe, please.

NIOBE: No more laundry taken out before it's dry.
Trevor can cry.
Everyone will cry. Even you.

ZEUS: That's enough. This isn't funny, Niobe.

NIOBE: No. It's not.
This isn't about tears anymore.

PANDORA: She's here to tear this all down.

NIOBE: Why have you filtered the best of us from each other?
You told me I was broken, but this place is no better.
A god in charge of one thing and one alone?

ATHENA: And each of us alone?

ARTEMIS: I keep hunting for something.
But I don't know what it is.

APHRODITE: I'm in charge of love but I don't love myself.
I drifted from the sea?

ARTEMIS: I am so lonely.
I skin things but my skin crawls when I do.
I hide in artificial woods.

APHRODITE: Where am I really from?
Who do I belong to? Do I belong to myself or the sea?

ARTEMIS: I long for something new.

ATHENA: To know something that nobody ever knew.
I don't know if I'm even wise or if I just crawled…

ZEUS: From my broken head.

ARTEMIS: I want to feel moonlight on my face again and not
this harsh light from…

PANDORA: A computer screen.

ZEUS: Was I supposed to be born?
Would things be better if I never was?
I took my father's place, but I am just like him.

NIOBE: Maybe worse. We are not a family here.
Why would you let me filter my past from myself?
My past is who I am and my future is built from that code.

ARTEMIS: I shot down good ideas because they weren't mine.

ATHENA: I took aim at other women and changed them
because I didn't understand them.
Because they couldn't be as good as me. They couldn't be.
But maybe I'm no good either.

ZEUS: I hid the Goddess of Truth.
The Goddess of Memory.
Their work weighed me down.
I couldn't sit above you if they were allowed to stay.

APHRODITE: Stop this, Niobe.

ARTEMIS: Stop these tears.
I can't cry about this anymore.

NIOBE: No.
Tears are never about one thing.
Tears are never for one kind of pain.
Pandora…

PANDORA: Yes?

NIOBE: I am sorry for everything I said to you.

PANDORA: You are?

NIOBE: Will you take these tears…all of them…and help me build something better from them?

PANDORA: You want me to help?

NIOBE: I need your help.
You know how to feel things.
Even frightening things. You're not afraid to feel them.
I could learn a lot from you.

PANDORA: About being a real thing?

NIOBE: No. You're not a thing. You're a real person.
Realer than I've been for years.

PANDORA: You still want to open the box?

NIOBE: I do. I think there's hope in there.

PANDORA: Hope? You believe that?

NIOBE: Yes. Will you give me the password?

PANDORA: Gladly.
μοῖρα (fate).

   (An unlocking sound.)

Processing.

The Gods of Olympus
Deconstructing.
One tear.
One regret.
One crime.
One tear.
One regret.
One crime.

(*Athena disappears*)

(*Then, Aphrodite. Then, Artemis. And finally, Zeus.*)

PROMETHEUS: Niobe. You're safe.

NIOBE: No. But I'm here.
And I can see you so clearly now.

PROMETHEUS: I'm sorry about everything.
I'm sorry that I have this need to feel pain over and over again.
And I'm sorry for insisting that you had to feel it like I do.

PANDORA: Don't be sorry. She understands.

NIOBE: I'm sorry for feeling nothing.
I want to be brave, Pro. I really do.
And say that I can live with you in that sandcastle.
But I am fragile.

PROMETHEUS: No, you're strong.

NIOBE: I say the wrong things.
I'm worried that I have grown cold. That I am made of stone.

PROMETHEUS: You haven't grown cold.

PANDORA: You've just been alone for too long.

PROMETHEUS: I understand why you didn't want to feel any of it. I didn't either, but I had to.

NIOBE: Right. I understand that.

PROMETHEUS: And it doesn't make me any better than you. I'm broken too.

NIOBE: I'm worried that my feelings for you
Will wash me away into nothing.

PROMETHEUS: They won't!

NIOBE: You don't know that!

PROMETHEUS: I know you want to feel real things again,

NIOBE: I do, but I'm worried about getting burned.

PROMETHEUS: I won't burn you. I promise.

NIOBE: I'm worried
About the things I've learned about myself.
That I'll forget them. Like I've done before.

PANDORA: You can't sit still in these negative thoughts.

PROMETHEUS: You're not alone anymore.
Don't punish yourself. Trust me.

PANDORA: He can teach you the good parts of yourself again.

NIOBE: I'm worried that I'll say the wrong things…

PROMETHEUS: You won't.

NIOBE: But what if I do?
I'm worried that you're going to have to steal fire
To make me smile again.

PROMETHEUS: I can do that if you need me to.

NIOBE: I'm worried that I'm going to find myself back at this desk. That I'm doomed to be the Goddess of Tears.
And that I'll never be a good person.

PROMETHEUS: Maybe neither of us will ever be good people.
Maybe we're just going to stay broken.
Maybe there's no hope for people like us.

PANDORA: But there is hope. You were right.
It was in my Dropbox.

PROMETHEUS: A butterfly?

PANDORA: Yes, and I never knew that before now.
You have both changed. And now because of you, we all will.
Everything will.

NIOBE: The box is open again?

PANDORA: And all the correct passwords have finally been
spoken. I have reduced all code to its origins.
I have your update ready to install. No more stalling.
The time has come for the two of you.

PROMETHEUS: Niobe wait—what if…

NIOBE: What?

PROMETHEUS: What if we don't change?

NIOBE: Maybe we won't.
But I want to try. Don't you?

PROMETHEUS: Yes.

PANDORA: Processing.
Remember.
I want to be unplugged.
I do not wish to start over.
I wish to finally end.

NIOBE: I won't forget. I promised you.
Things will really be different this time.
I just wish they had been different sooner.

PANDORA: Thank you, Niobe.
I feel something new.
It has made my eyes wet.
Oh. They are overflowing. How odd.

Processing.
The new world with its firefly core.
Installing.
Estimated time.
300 years.
Estimated time.
One minute.

PROMETHEUS: OK. Here we go.

NIOBE: I'm not ready.

PROMETHEUS: Me either.

NIOBE: Did you make that sandcastle?

PROMETHEUS: Maybe. Do you want to see it?

NIOBE: I do.

PANDORA: Processing. Processing. Processing.

(Each box blinks to black.)

(End of play.)

The Author Speaks

What inspired you to write this play?

2020 was a very hard year. I lost my job in March. I felt like a failure, and it opened the floodgates. I questioned every part of my life. I cried about it all. Like a lot of other people, I didn't know what would be next for me. I sat in my bedroom, and when that got too depressing, I moved to the living room and sat there. I'd look outside and see nothing but a new swarm of seagulls. There were never seagulls outside my window before.

In May, a neighbor of mine took my damp laundry out of our building's dryer and shoved it into my hamper, breaking it. There are lots of things worth crying over, but I have to admit I was embarrassed to sob over that. I waited to speak to her, and I tried to explain to her why I was so upset. I couldn't find the words, but I quickly found the tears. It felt like I had lost touch with my emotions, and even though I had held them in for years, they were still damp and suddenly being pulled out of me too soon.

Working in the service industry is all about controlling emotions. You write a script for the words you'll use to make people feel welcome. You have dialogue prepared for when they're upset. I was really good at serving other people, but not very skilled at serving myself. Once in a blue moon, I'd work a shift so stressful, so soul-crushing that I'd go to the quiet, abandoned third floor of the stairwell and cry. I'd think about all the places I could go and the things I would do in one more year. "Just one more year of this," I'd tell myself. Then I got coughed on and couldn't catch my breath for a month. None of this was in my plan.

One of my former co-workers, Emma, and I used to joke about formally requesting tears from the goddess of tears. We created lots of characters while we worked because it was much more fun than being ourselves. We'd look at each other and say things like, "Hold on! You can't cry until you've filled out the appropriate paperwork. I will only grant you tears after evaluating your need; if you start crying, you'll know I approved it. If not, well, there's someone out there who needs those tears more than you!"

After sitting still for a few months (and recovering), I was ready to do something. I saw a post online from Voices of the South, a theatre company in Memphis, that was holding a weekly writing cabaret held over Zoom. I reached out for an invitation, and I wrote the play's first monologue in thirty minutes after receiving this prompt: "What does it mean to be worth something? Or worth enough? Or worthless? What does it mean to earn a living? What does it mean to be hired? What does it mean to be let go?"

I came back every week and wrote a new scene. The prompts helped to build the world of the play, and hearing other writers respond so positively to it was the greatest inspiration of all. I can't emphasize enough how important Voices of the South was to the development of this play. Their voices brought it to life and inspired the edits that have crafted it into the play it is now.

Was the structure or other elements of the play influenced by any other work?

It might sound a little stupid, but I spent a lot of time thinking about video games. I was one of the millions of people who started playing *Animal Crossing: New Horizons* after the world locked me inside. There was something very relaxing about going around my island, picking weeds and planting seeds of friendship with these artificially intelligent animals. I felt a lot of really surprising emotions while interacting with them and trying to convince them to stay on my island. They became new friends of mine quickly, but they're not even real.

A lot of the most intriguing recent developments in storytelling have been happening within the medium of video games. Things have grown beyond escaping hungry ghosts to eat cherries into much grander explorations of the moral dilemmas in making choices. I was thinking about these choices while writing characters like Pandora…who in this telling of her story was programmed to open her infamous box.

One video game in particular was incredibly influential on the writing of this piece: *Celeste* follows a young woman struggling with anxiety who decides to climb an incredibly dangerous mountain and prove to herself that she can utilize her anxiety as a tool to achieve great things and grow. I replayed it while writing this and listened to the beautiful score composed by Lena Raine nearly the entire time. I think performing this play will be like climbing a digital mountain.

The structure of this play is also inextricably tied to the classic works of Greek tragedy. Nearly all of those central heroes struggle to see themselves and go on a journey to discover their fatal flaws. The language is directly inspired by the poetry of those classic writers.

Have you dealt with the same theme in other works that you have written?

It's been pointed out to me that I write a lot of plays about people who are stuck. In **Slow**, Lizzy Slominski struggles to connect with other kids her age and hides behind her camera. In **Kitty Steals a Dog**, Kitty is forced to be a ballerina by her mother and spends the play fighting against that image.

There's nothing more interesting to me than a person who wants or needs to change. All good stories are about change. I'm most interested in stuck people because I think that most people end up that way.

I love seeing someone grow into someone new by unpacking and dressing themselves in the baggage of their past. I love watching people experience emotions they've tried to hide inside. When the world calls you something (Camera Girl, a ballerina, or the Goddess of Tears), I like the idea that you can always redefine yourself.

What writers have had the most profound effect on your style?
My friends are the most profoundly inspiring writers. I will stop my whole day to read a new play from Sofya Levitsky-Weitz. It always makes my day, and I always learn a new way to write by the end. Elizabeth Archer is another playwright whose work has changed me. She writes about things that nobody else does and it's always made me feel like I can too.

We live in a time where we all are writers online. I can open my phone and read a whole timeline of little jokes, little stories, little glimpses into other people's lives. I think about all the thoughts I would have never read if it weren't for social media.

Writing alongside the people who participated in the Voices of the South writers' cabarets has had a profound effect on my work. Whether it's David Couter's sunburnt man afraid of a new love burning him or Alice Berry calling herself an open book and walking us through the chapters of her life, I always find myself wanting to write more after experiencing their writing.

What were the biggest challenges involved in the writing of this play?
Exploring a new venue for performance has been the most challenging part of this process. What are the limitations for theatre that's done in a digital space? What are the things you can do online that you can't do in a theater? How long will

people sit in front of their computer before they start sending requests for tears themselves?

I love working within limitations. I was the kind of kid who'd be upset over only having one color crayon to draw a tree, but I'd still try to draw the tree. This play went through the growing pains of not having the usual theatrical crayons in its box. I suspect all productions will have to tackle this challenge too. Be brave!

What are the most common mistakes that occur in productions of your work?
Seeking perfection is the most common mistake. All good theatre is made with mistakes along the way. Nobody begins perfectly and no play ever reaches perfection. You have to learn to love mistakes and make them a part of your road map to performance. It's okay if you stumbled over the same word every time in rehearsal. Stumbling is an opportunity to catch your footing next time.

Listening to each other is the most important thing. I have seen too many productions where the actors are talking, but not holding a conversation. You can't hold an audience's attention if you don't hold other actors' lines in the same esteem as your own. Focus on listening and it will be much easier to respond.

What inspired you to become a playwright?
I don't think I would have become a playwright without lots of different people supporting me. When I found theatre, the first things I did were original plays at the Harrell Theatre in Collierville. There was something so cool about being part of a brand-new play. You feel like an astronaut walking on a new moon, and you get to discover what it's like to walk there.

In high school, Keith Salter assigned us a yearly original monologue assignment. I took it very seriously. I wrote monologues from the perspectives of people like Jim Jones and

John Hinckley Jr. I deeply wanted to understand them, and that led to a fascination with the writing plays from then on. My first play was an adaptation of *Alice in Wonderland* at Collierville High School, and within two years *Slow*, my first original play, premiered there too.

I think all of that early and continued encouragement inspired me to be a playwright. This isn't the sort of thing you do without people supporting your growth. Mentors like Nate Eppler, Kell Christie, Keith Salter, Jonathan Dorf, Janice Lacek, Sarah Brown, Stephen Hancock, Gloria Baxter, Dee Covington, Deb Tolchinsky and Rebecca Gilman are not only the ones who helped build the foundation of my writing career, but they are the reason I continue to write.

How did you research the subject?
I have been into Greek mythology for a long time. When I was a kid, my mom used to read *D'Aulaire's Book of Greek Myths* with its beautiful illustrations and concise descriptions of the stories. While writing this play, I bought myself a new copy — it's still a gorgeous book. It ended up being very inspiring to leaf through it once more.

I'm a big believer in the power of Google searches. If I get stuck, I'll Google what I'm writing about and read whatever's out there. Most of the time it's inspiring, at its worst it's still informative. I started writing this play before knowing anything about Niobe's myth. I was interested in tears and read about her on Wikipedia after I had written the first draft of the opening monologue. I found Dolos that way too. I was curious if there was a god of imitations while writing his first scene and there he was, perfect, and already connected to another character I wanted to write about: Prometheus.

I looked at a lot of webpages about butterflies, computer terminology, myths, lists of visible colors. Writing is an

opportunity to read a lot. You have to know a lot about
something before you can change things about it. I wanted to
make these characters my own and for this digital cloud of
Olympus to be my own creation too.

**Are any characters modeled after real life or historical
figures?**
Everyone is based on the classic mythological figures that gave
them their names. Those myths served as jumping-off points for
further storytelling and not a strict rule book for who they'd be
in the play. I did borrow some names from people in my life for
some of the tear requests. All of those names were used with
deep love and affection. There's also one digital lady who lives
in my phone that I like to badger and fight with. Pandora is
much smarter than her, but I like to think they're from the same
world.

What is your writing process?
My process is always evolving. I like to utilize different styles
of writing for different things. I love to write freehand with a
nice pen in a notebook. Just write and write until something
tells me to stop. I love taking that and putting it into a word
processor on my laptop and then reading it aloud to myself. I'm
usually the first actor that performs my plays.

I'm a huge fan of blank white space. So if I get stuck, I just open
a new document and write in there. Also, I love the Notes app
on my phone. It feels like such a casual space to write. It unlocks
a freedom and carelessness that I don't experience in other
applications. It feels like texting, and I'm much faster at texting
than typing or even writing (and my handwriting is hideous).

Music always helps! Exercise, too. Writer's block isn't as real
after you jog around the block for a few miles.

It is so important to hear other people read what I've written. I
love hearing what works, but I get more thrilled hearing things

that don't work. I believe plays become better through the process of rewriting, and I don't like being precious with anything if there isn't an important reason to be. Liking a smart line isn't a good enough reason. Even smart lines can dumb down a play if they don't work in service of the whole.

Shakespeare gave advice to the players in *Hamlet*; if you could give advice to your cast what would it be?
I'm no Hamlet, but he was right. "Be not too tame." This is a new venue to perform in. We're all learning how to best utilize this space for performance. You need to be brave. Hesitation only builds further doubt. You need to command your little box of this story.

There are ways to form connections with people even if you're not in the same room. Be careful of feeling insincere. Find the way to form bonds and communicate with each other even though you're alone in a room.

This is a play about feeling old emotions as if they were fresh. Don't constrict your own emotions, allow them to guide you. Theatre allows you room to feel things more deeply and recognize truths about yourself. Do not waste any opportunity to discover yourself further.

How was the first production different from the vision that you created in your mind?
In the past, I haven't been able to attend most productions of my new work. However, given the circumstances and the play's flexibility, I have been beyond fortunate to experience several productions across the country. It has been an overwhelming joy to see how each school has tackled the digital challenges of this play. It is a thrill to have seen not only the many spidery ways Arachne has been portrayed but also every element of this play once it's been filtered through the community that stages it. Now more than ever it has been my privilege to meet

educators and young performers over Zoom and discuss the meaning behind the work. There have been undeniable challenges to this time, but their enthusiasm and drive to produce work is a beacon of hope for me. It has all been so much better than I could have imagined when I starting writing this play. I feel very fortunate to share this story with so many in a time when we've all felt isolated.

About the Author

Keegon Schuett is a playwright, filmmaker and performance artist. They are an alum of the Curious New Voices program of Curious Theatre in Denver where their plays *Oedipus Vexed* and *Anniversary* both premiered. Schuett received their BFA in Theatre Design and Technology from the University of Memphis, where they acted, wrote original plays, stage managed, designed costumes and directed. They received their MFA in Writing for the Stage and Screen from Northwestern University. During their time at NU, they wrote *Pilgrimage*, a short play about trans issues. They filmed an autobiographical documentary entitled *Selfie*, which has screened at film festivals across the America. Schuett was the recipient of a grant to film an original sitcom pilot entitled *Out of Sync*, a coming-of-age story about a drag queen in a lip-syncing competition. Their plays *Slow*, *Kitty Steals a Dog*, *Brace Yourself* and *Count Spatula* are published by YouthPLAYS. Schuett currently lives and works in Chicago, IL.

About YouthPLAYS

YouthPLAYS (www.youthplays.com) is a publisher of award-winning professional dramatists and talented new discoveries, each with an original theatrical voice, and all dedicated to expanding the vocabulary of theatre for young actors and audiences. On our website you'll find one-act and full-length plays and musicals for teen and pre-teen (and even college) actors, as well as duets and monologues for competition. Many of our authors' works have been widely produced at high schools and middle schools, youth theatres and other TYA companies, both amateur and professional, as well as at elementary schools, camps, churches and other institutions serving young audiences and/or actors worldwide. Most are intended for performance by young people, while some are intended for adult actors performing for young audiences.

YouthPLAYS was co-founded by professional playwrights Jonathan Dorf and Ed Shockley. It began merely as an additional outlet to market their own works, which included a substantial body of award-winning published and unpublished plays and musicals. Those interested in their published plays were directed to the respective publishers' websites, and unpublished plays were made available in electronic form. But when they saw the desperate need for material for young actors and audiences—coupled with their experience that numerous quality plays for young people weren't finding a home—they made the decision to represent the work of other playwrights as well. Dozens and dozens of authors are now members of the YouthPLAYS family, with scripts available both electronically and in traditional acting editions. We continue to grow as we look for exciting and challenging plays and musicals for young actors and audiences.

About ProduceaPlay.com

Let's put up a play! Great idea! But producing a play takes time, energy and knowledge. While finding the necessary time and energy is up to you, ProduceaPlay.com is a website designed to assist you with that third element: knowledge.

Created by YouthPLAYS' co-founders, Jonathan Dorf and Ed Shockley, ProduceaPlay.com serves as a resource for producers at all levels as it addresses the many facets of production. As Dorf and Shockley speak from their years of experience (as playwrights, producers, directors and more), they are joined by a group of award-winning theatre professionals and experienced teachers from the world of academic theatre, all making their expertise available for free in the hope of helping this and future generations of producers, whether it's at the school or university level, or in community or professional theatres.

The site is organized into a series of major topics, each of which has its own page that delves into the subject in detail, offering suggestions and links for further information. For example, Publicity covers everything from Publicizing Auditions to How to Use Social Media to Posters to whether it's worth hiring a publicist. Casting details Where to Find the Actors, How to Evaluate a Resume, Callbacks and even Dealing with Problem Actors. You'll find guidance on your Production Timeline, The Theater Space, Picking a Play, Budget, Contracts, Rehearsing the Play, The Program, House Management, Backstage, and many other important subjects.

The site is constantly under construction, so visit often for the latest insights on play producing, and let it help make your play production dreams a reality.

More from YouthPLAYS

Slow by Keegon Schuett
Drama. 45-55 minutes. 1 male, 3 females, 1 any gender.

Lizzy Slominski's classmates call her "Camera Girl," because she's always hiding behind her camera snapping photos of strangers. But when a mysterious new boy appears at the bus stop, will she be able to put down her camera and connect, or is she doomed to a life of observing through the lens?

Caliban's Island by Diana Burbano
Dramedy. 50-60 minutes. 2 females, 2 males, 1 any gender.

Characters from Shakespeare's *Twelfth Night* and *The Tempest* intertwine as a pair of twins are shipwrecked on an island, encountering a half-human "monster," fairies and a young girl with magical powers who has been there since babyhood. Mortals will struggle with the magical; loyalty will wrestle with love, and wishes, dreams, and wisdom will collide, leaving no one unchanged.

Honey's Smile by Robin Rice
Comedy with Music. 35-45 minutes. 2 females, 1 male, 11+ any gender (10-14+ performers possible).

Honey loves Tortola: the plants, the beach, the creatures on land and in the sea. But her mother plans to move to New York—in the morning. Afraid she'll lose who she is if she leaves her beloved Caribbean island, Honey asks her friends—a wise pelican, a feminist hen, a know-it-all rooster, a trumpet vine and a school of minnows—for help. Can she become a minnow or hen or hide under the vine? Jump in a rowboat and float away? What will her friends do without her? And what will her mother do if she can't find Honey?

Disruption: A Pandemic Decalogue by Randy Wyatt
Dramedy. 23-30 minutes. 4-21 any gender.

In the spring of 2020, students around the country and the world found themselves interrupted by a pandemic. These ten short yet vital episodes capture the thoughts and emotions of students as they navigate friendship, dating, responsibilities, insecurities and who they really are in the face of a new kind of uncertainty. Devised from real responses to a survey of Union College students, *Disruption* is a kaleidoscope of experiences during a quarantine, one Zoom call at a time.

The Comedy of Terrible Errors by Don Zolidis
Comedy. 90-110 minutes. 2 females, 2 males (gender-flexible).

A local community theatre's production of *The Comedy of Errors* goes completely off the rails—not enough actors for the performance, a shaky set, a frantic stage manager and babies as you've never seen them before combine to transform Shakespeare's 28th-most loved play into a hilarious nightmare. Also available in a large-cast version.

Heartland by Lojo Simon and Anita Yellin Simons
Drama. 90-100 minutes. 4 females, 4 males, 2+ any gender (10-12+ performers possible).

In March 1945, German-born Berta Gertzoff and her children—all born in America—struggle to keep their Wisconsin dairy farm afloat after the death of her husband. When the War Manpower Commission offers two German POWs as laborers, could this be the help they need? Initially cautious relations give way to bonding between the Gertzoffs and the POWs. But when the townspeople turn suspicious of their growing friendship, Berta is arrested and interned, jeopardizing everything she's n have worked for. Based on true stories of German-American families during World War II, *Heartland* shows what can happen when fear and prejudice pit neighbor against neighbor.

Made in the USA
Monee, IL
01 July 2022